# IELTS *express*

## Intermediate

### Coursebook

Richard Hallows

Martin Lisboa

Mark Unwin

**THOMSON**
™

Australia • Canada • Mexico • Singapore • Spain • United Kingdom • United States

## IELTS Express Intermediate, Coursebook
Hallows / Lisboa / Unwin

**Publisher:** *Christopher Wenger*
**Director of Product Development:** *Anita Raducanu*
**Director of Product Marketing:** *Amy Mabley*
**Editorial Manager:** *Sean Bermingham*
**Development Editor:** *Derek Mackrell*
**Production Editor:** *Tan Jin Hock*
**International Marketing Manager:** *Ian Martin*
**Sr. Print Buyer:** *Mary Beth Hennebury*
**Project Manager:** *Howard Middle/HM ELT Services*
**Production Management:** *Process ELT (www.process-elt.com)*

**Contributing Writers:** *Mark Harrison, Pamela Humphreys, Russell Whitehead*
**Copy Editor:** *Georgia Zographou/Process ELT*
**Compositor:** *Process ELT*
**Illustrators:** *Nick Dimitriadis, Oxford Designers & Illustrators, Peter Standley*
**Cover/Text Designer:** *Studio Image & Photographic Art (www.studio-image.com)*
**Printer:** *G. Canale & C S.p.a.*
**Cover Image:** *Michael Dunning/Getty Images*

ISBN: 1-4130-0955-7

### Text Credits
Page 58: From "The Shape of Things to Come." Copyright © 2003 THE ECONOMIST. Page 88: From "The Constant Turn-on," by Jackie Holland. Copyright © Telegraph Group Limited 2004. Page 92: From "Howl of Wolves Nears U.S. Suburbs," by James Gorman. Copyright © 2004 by the New York Times Co. Page 94: From "Mars... a Big Step for Womankind?" by Raj Persaud. Copyright © Telegraph Group Limited 2004. Page 97: Copyright © Verdict Research Ltd. 2004. Page 101: Leaflet produced by the London Borough of Barnet. Page 102: Reproduced with permission of the Science Museum, London Page 103: From Southgate College Prospectus, 2004–2005. Copyright © Southgate College. Page 104: From Barnet College Prospectus, 2004–2005. Copyright © Barnet College. Page 105: From "Playing with Matches Could Be Good for Your Wealth," by Robert Miller. Copyright © Telegraph Group Limited 2003.

### Photo Credits
Page 8, left © IT Stock Free, right © BananaStock; page 10 © Brand X Pictures; page 12 © Index Stock/Walter Bibikow; page 13, left © IT Stock Free, right © Image Source Limited; page 16, top left © Novastock, top right © Index Stock/David Shopper, bottom left © AbleStock, bottom right © Index Stock/Peter Cross; page 20 © Index Stock/Jon Riley; page 24, top left © Creatas, bottom left © Index Stock/Lou Jones, middle © Digital Vision, right © Photodisc; page 26, photo 1 © Index Stock/Doug Mazell, photo 2 © Digital Vision, photo 3 © Creatas, photo 4 © RubberBall Productions; page 29 © Digital Vision; page 37 © Stockbyte; page 40 © Stock Connection; page 42 © Index Stock Imagery; page 45 © Powerstock; page 48 © Index Stock/Donald Higgs; page 51, top © Index Stock/Sally Brown, middle © AP Photo/Ed Reinke, bottom © AP Photo/Tom Uhlman; page 52, left © Stock Connection, top right © Index Stock/Peter Adams, bottom right © ImageState; page 56, left © Photodisc, right © Great American Stock; page 57 © Index Stock/John James Wood; page 61 © Creatas; page 64 © ImageState; page 68, left © Index Stock/Tom Stillo, right © PhotoAlto; page 72, left © BananaStock, right © Digital Vision; page 76 © Image Source; page 78, top left © ThinkStock LLC, top right © photolibrary.com, bottom © Photodisc; page 79 © PhotoAlto; page 80 © Goodshoot

### Author Acknowledgements
The authors would like to jointly thank Sean Bermingham and Derek Mackrell for their considerable creative input, hard work and sheer dedication to this project, Howard Middle, project consultant for his superb problem solving skills, and Chris Wenger the publisher for his good humour and showing us all a good time. We would also like to thank Loukas Ioannou and Georgia Zographou for their warm hospitality in Athens and help with development ideas for the book.

*Martin:* A big thank you to colleagues and students at the English Language Centre, London Metropolitan University for trialling material and offering sound advice and support. To my wife Manuela and my son Max, a very special thank you for tolerating me spending far too much time in front of the computer screen – without your support, good humour and inspiration, this book would have been impossible.

*Richard:* I'd like to thank my parents and friends, especially the Simons, who have supported me through this amazing project.

*Mark:* In addition to our wonderful editors and designers ... I'd like to thank my wife Sarah, my family, everyone whose brains I've picked over the last two years (they know who they are) and finally every student I've ever had in my class and every teacher whose class I've ever been in.

# What is IELTS?

IELTS (International English Language Testing System) is a globally recognised English language exam, designed to assess the language ability of candidates who need to study or work where English is the language of communication. It is accepted by the majority of universities and further education colleges in the UK, Australia, Ireland, New Zealand, Canada, South Africa as well as a large number of institutions in the United States. It is also recognised by professional bodies, immigration authorities and other government agencies. IELTS is jointly managed by the University of Cambridge ESOL Examinations (Cambridge ESOL), the British Council and IDP: IELTS Australia.

IELTS is offered in two formats – Academic and General Training. All candidates take the same Listening and Speaking modules and there is an option of either Academic or General Training Reading and Writing modules. Academic is suitable for students wishing to enter an undergraduate or postgraduate study programme. General Training is suitable for candidates planning to undertake non-academic training, or work experience, or for immigration purposes.

Further information about the exam can be obtained from the IELTS website www.ielts.org.

# What is the *IELTS Express* series?

*IELTS Express* is a two-level exam preparation course at Intermediate level (IELTS grade 4–5.5) and Upper Intermediate level (IELTS grade 5 and above). The *IELTS Express* series focuses on building skills and providing essential exam practice. In addition to the Coursebook, each level of *IELTS Express* comprises the following components:

### Workbook

The Workbook contains vocabulary and grammar tasks, skills building tasks and exam practice tasks. It is suitable for classroom or self-study use, and is accompanied by a separate audio component for additional speaking and listening practice.

### Teacher's Guide

The Teacher's Guide provides detailed guidance on how to approach the Coursebook tasks and suggestions about extending these tasks. In addition, there are notes on how to adapt the material according to the level of your students. Practice test answers and model essays for the writing tasks are also included. The Teacher's Guides are designed for both experienced teachers of IELTS and teachers who are unfamiliar with the exam.

### Video/DVD

The Video/DVD shows students taking a simulated IELTS speaking exam with an IELTS examiner. It includes commentary from the examiner on the candidates' performance, with particular reference to the skills practised in the speaking sections of the Coursebook.

### Audio Tapes/CDs

The Audio Tapes/CDs contain all the recorded material from the Coursebook, including listening tasks and model answers for all the speaking sections.

*IELTS Express* is designed to work flexibly for courses of any length. For short courses, the Coursebook can be used to provide approximately 30–40 hours teaching time. For longer courses, *IELTS Express Intermediate* and *IELTS Express Upper Intermediate Coursebooks* can be taught consecutively, providing approximately 60–80 hours teaching time. This can be further extended if combined with *IELTS Express Workbooks* and *Videos/DVDs*.

## IELTS Express Intermediate

### How is the book organised?

The book is divided into eight theme-based units covering a broad range of typical IELTS topic areas. Each unit covers one productive skill and one receptive skill. Units 1, 3, 5 and 7 consist of a Reading and Speaking section, while Units 2, 4, 6, and 8 consist of a Listening and Writing section.

*IELTS Express Intermediate Coursebook* also includes:

- a separate section on the **General Training Writing module**
- a complete **Practice test** for both Academic and General Training modules
- an **Answer key**
- **Listening scripts** for all the recorded material
- a **Language bank** of useful expressions for the speaking and writing exam tasks

### How is each unit section organised?

Each unit section (Reading, Speaking, Listening and Writing) consists of the following:

- an **Introduction** which presents the topic through discussion questions and/or a task on key vocabulary
- **skills development** tasks
- **exam practice** tasks
- an **In the exam** box which gives detailed information on a particular part or section of the exam
- **For this task** boxes which offer step-by-step guidance and general strategies for tackling each task
- **Express tips** which highlight points to remember when taking the exam

Each writing section includes a **model essay** and each speaking section includes an **audio recording** of a model answer. The models are graded to provide students with an aspirational, yet realistic goal to aim for.

### How can *Express Intermediate* be used by both Academic and General Training module candidates?

*IELTS Express Intermediate* offers preparation for both versions of the test – Academic and General Training. Students preparing for the **Academic** module can:

- work though Units 1–8
- refer to the relevant sections of the Language bank
- do the Practice test for the Academic module

Students preparing for the **General Training** module can:

- work through Units 1–8
- do Units GT 1A and GT 1B, **instead of** Unit 2 and Unit 6 writing sections
- do Unit GT 2
- refer to the relevant sections of the Language bank
- do the Practice test for the General Training module

# Acknowledgements

The authors and publishers would like to thank all those who participated in the development of the project:

Gill Atkinson, The British Council, Singapore

Elizabeth Au, The British Council, Kuala Lumpur, Malaysia

Lucas Bak, The British Council, Seoul, Korea

Julia Boardwell, PLAN, Nagoya, Japan

Crispin Davies, EF, Cambridge, England

Belinda Hardisty, Studio Cambridge, Cambridge, England

Lee Hewson, The British Council, Hanoi, Vietnam

Kirsten Holt, St. Giles International, Eastbourne, England

Carmel Milroy, The British Council, Hanoi, Vietnam

Katherine Morris, The British Council, Naples, Italy

Karima Moyer, Universita' di Siena, Siena, Italy

Daniela Panayotova, EF, Cambridge, England

Guy Perring, The British Council, Tokyo, Japan

Vincent Smidowicz, Sidmouth International School, Sidmouth, England

Colin Thorpe, The British Council, Seoul, Korea

Emma Wheeler, The British Council, Hong Kong

Ying Xiong, Beijing New Oriental School, Beijing, China


In addition, the authors and publishers would like to express their gratitude to Mark Harrison, Pamela Humphreys and Russell Whitehead for their invaluable contribution to the series.

# IELTS *express*
## TABLE OF CONTENTS

**IELTS Exam summary:** Inside front flap
**Language bank:** Inside back flap

# Studying Overseas

> **Exam tasks** ▶ Short-answer questions; classification; true/false/not given
> **Skills** ▶ Skimming and scanning; predicting content

## 1 Introduction

Discuss these questions with a partner.

- Have you ever studied abroad? Where did you study? Did you enjoy it? What were the main benefits of studying abroad? What were the main challenges?
- If you have never studied abroad, would you like to? Where and what would you like to study? Why? What do you think are the main benefits of studying abroad? What do you think would be the main challenges?

## 2 Skimming and scanning

**A** Both skimming and scanning involve reading a text quickly, but are used for different reasons. Skimming is when you quickly read for just the main idea of a text, without thinking about specific details. Scanning is when you read to find specific pieces of information, such as names, dates and facts. Look at situations 1–4 below and tick the correct box for each.

### IN THE EXAM

**Reading module: Academic and General Training**

The IELTS Reading module takes 60 minutes and consists of three sections. In the Academic module, each section features one reading text taken from books, magazines, journals and newspapers. In the General Training module, each section may consist of one or more passages, taken from sources such as advertisements, leaflets and instruction manuals, of the kind you would find every day in an English-speaking country.

In both the Academic and General Training modules, you have to answer 40 questions in total, based on a variety of task types, such as matching, short-answer questions, true/false/not given and multiple-choice questions. The task types and skills required for them (skimming, scanning, making predictions, etc.) are the same for the Academic and General Training modules.

|  | skim | scan |
|---|:---:|:---:|
| 1 You look at a newspaper to see if there's a film on TV tonight. | ❑ | ❑ |
| 2 You look at a train timetable to see when the next train is due. | ❑ | ❑ |
| 3 You need to decide if a long article will be useful for some research you are doing. | ❑ | ❑ |
| 4 You have a meeting in ten minutes, and you haven't read the report you are going to discuss. | ❑ | ❑ |

**B** Skim the short article below in 30 seconds. Which of the following describes the main idea of the text?

1 It is important to speak English if you want to be successful in business.

2 Most of the world's mail is written in English.

3 English is the most widely used language in the world.

> English is the second most commonly spoken, and by far the most widespread of the world's languages. It is estimated that there are 300 million native speakers, 300 million who use English as a second language and a further billion using it as a foreign language. English is spoken by scientists, pilots, computer experts, diplomats and tourists; it is the language of the world! Did you know over 50% of all business deals are conducted in English? And over 70% of all mail is written and addressed in English? It is the official or co-official language of over 45 countries and furthermore, it is spoken extensively in other countries where it has no official status. It is perhaps, therefore, not surprising that in recent years we have seen a dramatic increase in the number of students opting to study abroad. In the future this will cement the role that English plays in the cultural, political or economic life of many countries around the world from Australia to Zambia.

**C** Look at these numbers from the text. Do you remember what they refer to? Match the numbers with their reference below. Then scan the text in 30 seconds to find the answers.

over 70%                                    the amount of business done in English

over 50%                                    the amount of mail written in English

## 3 Predicting content

**A** Before you read a text in the IELTS exam, it is a good idea to predict what you are going to read. One way is to use the information in the title (or main heading), the summary paragraph and any subheadings.

Look at the article on page 10. Read the main heading and the subheadings. Based on the information in the headings, which of the following do you think best describes the text?

1 Information about universities, promoting each institution as a good place to study

2 A holiday brochure, 'selling' the UK as a destination for a quick break

3 A magazine article, giving advice on living and studying abroad in different English-speaking countries

**B** When you skim a text, don't worry about words you don't understand. Try to get an overall impression of the text. Make sure you read the first sentence of each paragraph. These will help you get an overview of the text. Time yourself, and take two minutes to skim the article. Then decide if your answer in 3A was correct.

# Your adventure starts where?

**An increasing number of students are thinking of going overseas to study for a degree. This week we focus on five English-speaking countries, examining what each has to offer and why you might choose to study there.**

With thousands of institutions and courses to choose from, how do you decide where to study as an international student? Do you dream of heading for the land of Uncle Sam or would you feel more at home in Shakespeare's country? Perhaps the Australian outback will give you the space you need to work out the problems of the world. Whichever you choose, the adventure begins right here!

## STUDY IN AUSTRALIA

Free-spirited Australia has been open to migration for many years and is today one of the world's top three destinations for international students. Australia's renowned cultural diversity, its high level of public safety and the vibrant atmosphere of its cities all help to make it easy for overseas visitors to feel at home. Academically speaking, most of the national, publicly-funded universities are of similarly high standard. Moreover, Australian institutions have a particularly strong reputation for research into the environment and sport science.

## STUDY IN THE UK

Many students are attracted to Britain by its long history of literature, from Chaucer and Shakespeare to Bridget Jones and Harry Potter. Look beyond this, and you'll find a university system with one of the best reputations in the world. Universities in the UK have a record of achievement in business, law, the sciences, philosophy, linguistics and many other fields. Some UK institutions offer a foundation course (usually three months or one year in length) to prepare international students before they go on to do a full undergraduate degree; applying for one of these courses normally involves taking the IELTS exam.

## STUDY IN NEW ZEALAND

With its vast and beautiful open spaces and friendly city centres, New Zealand is a country where you can enjoy both the great outdoors and the conveniences and dynamism of modern city life. Low living costs and a high standard of living also make life here very appealing. New Zealand's highly respected educational programmes are based on the British system. A large part of a degree programme is practical; this gives graduates both the knowledge and the skills they need when entering the workplace.

## STUDY IN THE USA

The population of the US is made up of people from every continent, joined together by a shared language and a core set of values. Of these values, liberty and freedom are probably the most important, combined with individual responsibility. American students are therefore expected to think independently and have responsibility for their own studies; classes are often informal and students are encouraged to express their opinion. With 50 States all offering a huge range of different types of institutions – from two-year community college courses to four-year undergraduate programmes – deciding where to study in the US may appear confusing, so it is important to do some research first.

## STUDY IN CANADA

Surveys conducted by the United Nations have repeatedly found Canada to be among the top three places in the world to live in. In addition, Canada's largest cities, Vancouver, Toronto and Montreal, have been recognised as world-class cities in which to live and work, for their cleanliness and safety and for their cultural activities and attractive lifestyles. A Canadian degree, diploma or certificate is well regarded in business, government and academic circles around the globe. Canada has two official languages – English and French. Studying and living in Canada could be your opportunity to learn both!

## 4 Short-answer questions

Short-answer questions ask you to write one, two or three words for each question. If your answer is too long or uses different words to those in the passage, it will be marked as incorrect.

For each question:

▸ First, decide what kind of information you need to answer the question. Is it a *where*, *when*, *what*, *which* or *who* question? Then look for keywords (most important words) in the question, for example, personal names, places and dates.

▸ Scan the headings in the passage to help you find the relevant part of the text. Then scan that section of the passage for possible answers (or to confirm your predicted answer).

▸ Check that your answer fits the maximum word count. Remember to use words taken directly from the passsage. Don't change the form of the words or use different words.

*Questions 1–5*

*Answer the following questions. Write* **NO MORE THAN THREE WORDS** *for each answer.*

1  What type of university preparation course is available in the UK?  ........................

2  On which education system are New Zealand programmes founded?  ........................

3  Which two values are extremely important to Americans?  ........................

4  Which US educational programmes are two years in length?  ........................

5  Who concluded that Canada is one of the best countries in the world to live in?  ........................

## 5 Classification

In classification tasks, you will see a list of categories and a number of statements. You need to match the statements with the correct categories according to the passage. The statements will be paraphrased; they will have the same meaning as the information in the text, but they may be worded differently. Sometimes the number of categories is the same as the number of statements, but not always.

▸ Skim the passage to decide which section of the passage each category (in this case each country) refers to.

▸ Read the first statement and scan the sections of the passage you identified to find an idea that has the same meaning. Note the letters that correspond to that country.

▸ Repeat the process for the rest of the statements.

*Questions 6–10*

*Which countries do the following statements refer to? Choose your answers from the box and write the correct letters next to questions 6–10.*

| | |
|---|---|
| **AU** | Australia |
| **CA** | Canada |
| **NZ** | New Zealand |
| **UK** | United Kingdom |
| **US** | United States |

**express tip**

The categories will be listed in a logical order, for example, alphabetically. Be careful because the categories may not match the order in which they appear in the text.

6  There is an enormous choice of colleges and universities to choose from.  ........................

7  Some universities are famous for courses in environmental studies.  ........................

8  It is well-known for producing many famous authors.  ........................

9  Students should be able to think for themselves.  ........................

10  It is not a very expensive place to live in.  ........................

## 6 True/False/Not Given

### for this task

True/False/Not Given questions ask you to read statements and compare them to the information given in the passage. You need to decide if the statement is true or false according to the passage. If the statement relates to information given in the passage, but the passage doesn't actually agree or disagree with the statement, you need to select 'Not Given'.

▶ Read the first statement. Look for keywords that can help you decide which part of the passage to focus on.

Then skim the passage to find the relevant section.

▶ Read the information in that section of the passage carefully. If the idea expressed in the passage is the same as the statement, answer 'True'. If the passage disagrees with the statement, answer 'False'. If the passage contains information relating to the statement, but doesn't actually agree or disagree with it, answer 'Not Given'.

▶ Repeat the process for the rest of the statements.

**Questions 11–15**

*Do the following statements agree with the information given in the passage? Next to questions 11–15 write*

**TRUE**          *if the statement agrees with the information*
**FALSE**         *if the statement contradicts the information*
**NOT GIVEN**  *if there is no information on this*

11  Australia is a dangerous country.                                    ...........
12  Most state universities in Australia are of comparable quality.      ...........
13  A degree from a UK university is highly regarded.                    ...........
14  The British education system has a large practical element.          ...........
15  Canada has the top three universities in the world.                  ...........

▸ **Exam focus** ▸ Speaking Part 1: Introduction and interview
▸ **Skills** ▸ Answering questions about yourself; extending your responses

## 1 Introduction

**A** Look at the photographs of people meeting for the first time. What questions do you think they are asking each other? Make a list of typical questions people ask each other when meeting for the first time.

**B** Now ask your partner some of these questions. Try to find out a little about him or her.

## 2 Answering questions about yourself

**A** Look at conversations 1–6 between speaker A and speaker B below. Read speaker B's responses. What question do you think speaker A has asked? Discuss with a partner.

1 **A** ................................................................?

 **B**(a) ............ I don't like it very much. I think it's really difficult, especially the grammar.

2 **A** ................................................................?

 **B**(b) ............ I often go out with my friends, but sometimes I enjoy just reading in my room.

### IN THE EXAM

**Speaking module: Part 1**

The Speaking exam consists of three parts, which are the same for both the Academic and General Training modules. In Part 1, the examiner will ask you questions about yourself, such as your city or town, work or study, your family, your free time, your reasons for learning English and your plans for the future.

The questions in Part 1 are about you and your personal experience and opinions. You will be evaluated on fluency and coherence, range of vocabulary, grammatical range and accuracy and pronunciation.

Part 1 lasts about four to five minutes.

**3 A** .........................................?

**B** I haven't really decided yet. (c) ............ I'd like to one day, maybe in Canada or Australia.

**4 A** .........................................?

**B**(d) ............ , I have one brother and one sister.

**5 A** .........................................?

**B** I have a part-time job in a local shop. (e) ............ , I've worked there for more than three years.

**6 A** .........................................?

**B**(f) ............ , my parents moved around a lot and I've lived in many cities. Now I live in Osaka.

**B** 🎧 **1.1** Listen to the conversations and write down the questions that were asked.

**C** 🎧 **1.1** Listen again and write the missing words or expressions (a–f) in speaker B's response in each conversation.

**D** Write words or expressions a–f in the table below. Then match each one with its function.

express tip

Using words or expressions like actually, well or it depends will make you sound more natural when you speak.

| Expression | Function |
| --- | --- |
| a ...... *I'm afraid* ...... | **i** I'm going to give extra information about my response. |
| b ........................... | **ii** I think so or I suppose so. |
| c ........................... | **iii** I'm going to apologise or disagree politely. |
| d ........................... | **iv** I can't give you a simple answer. |
| e ........................... | **v** Wait a second. I'm thinking. |
| f ........................... | **vi** I'm going to tell you something surprising or interesting. |

**E** Ask and answer questions 1–6 in a way that is true for yourself. Try to use some of the expressions in the table above.

## 3 Extending your responses

**A** To demonstrate your English ability to the examiner, it is important to give full responses. Instead of giving short, one- or two-word answers, try to extend your responses by providing two or three additional pieces of information. Look at the example below.

**Examiner:** 'Do you plan to study abroad?'

**Candidate:** 'Yes, I do. I hope to go to Ireland, to Dublin. I want to study medicine. People say the universities there are very good for this subject.'

**B** One way to extend your answers is to try asking yourself follow-up questions. This will help you think of additional information you can use in your response. Read the question below and with your partner, think of follow-up questions. Then take turns answering the question, using your follow-up questions to extend your answers.

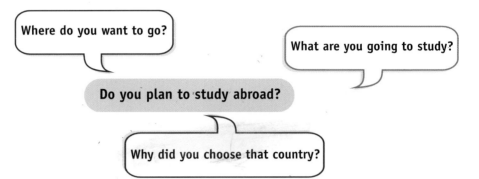

**Where do you want to go?**

**What are you going to study?**

**Do you plan to study abroad?**

**Why did you choose that country?**

**C** Write a short answer for each of the questions below. Then extend your answer by adding two or three pieces of information. Your answers don't have to be full sentences. They can be notes.

1  Do have any brothers or sisters?
2  Where do you live?
3  What do you do in your free time?
4  Do you enjoy studying English?
5  What's your job?
6  Do you plan to study abroad?

......................................................................
......................................................................
......................................................................
......................................................................
......................................................................
......................................................................

**express tip**

Use words like *also, so* and *because* to join your ideas when you speak.

 **D** **1.2** Listen to some students answering questions 1–6 above.

1  What extra information does each student provide? Write down the keywords as you listen.
2  What were the follow-up questions that they asked themselves?

## 4  Introduction and interview

### for this task

In the beginning of Part 1, the examiner will greet you and ask for your name and some identification. Then, you will be asked questions about yourself and your life.

▸ Listen to the examiner's questions carefully. Remember to extend your answers.

▸ Use expressions like *well, actually* and *I guess*, and linking words like *so* and *because* to connect your ideas and sound more fluent.

▸ Continue speaking even if you have made a mistake.

Work with a partner. In pairs, role-play Part 1 of the Speaking exam.

**Student A:** You are the examiner. Choose some questions from 3C above. For each question, think of follow-up questions (*why, when, where, who with,* etc.) and interview student B for four or five minutes. Listen to student B's answers carefully. Did he or she give short or extended responses?

**Student B:** You are the candidate. Imagine you are in the exam. Introduce yourself briefly and then listen to the examiner's questions. Answer as fully as possible, giving two or three additional pieces of information for each question. Follow the advice in *for this task*.
When you have finished, change roles with your partner.

# **2** Shopping and the Internet

> ▸ **Exam tasks** ▸ Form completion; notes completion
> ▸ **Exam focus** ▸ Listening Section 1: Non-academic dialogue
> ▸ **Skills** ▸ Imagining the situation and language; identifying the question; identifying the answer type

## **1** Introduction

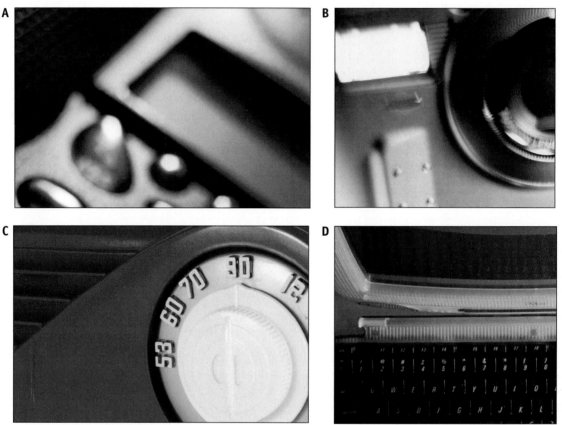

Discuss these questions with a partner.

- Can you identify the items in pictures A–D? Have you ever bought any of these items?

- When people buy one of the items in the photos, what kind of questions do they ask the sales assistant? What kind of questions does the sales assistant ask them? Make a list of these questions.

- What kind of forms would someone buying these items have to complete? What kind of information would they have to provide?

## IN THE EXAM

### Listening module: Section I

The Listening module takes about 30 minutes and consists of four sections, which are the same for both Academic and General Training candidates.

Section I is a non-academic dialogue. Two speakers have a discussion in a social situation, such as arranging an appointment, buying goods or services, etc. The conversation is about two minutes long and you will hear it only once.

Completion tasks are quite common in Section I. In notes completion and form completion tasks, you are presented with a form or set of notes which are only partly completed and you are asked to fill in the missing information using words and/or a number.

## 2 Imagining the situation and language

**A** In the exam, each different listening situation is introduced on the recording. For example, you may hear the following:

*'You will hear a customer enquiring about buying a camera.'*

You should then spend a few seconds before the dialogue begins thinking about the kind of situation you are about to hear and the kind of language that may be used.

Where do you think this conversation is taking place? Who are the people talking? What questions do you think you will hear? What vocabulary related to the situation do you think you may hear?

**B** **2.1** Now listen to the recording and check if your predictions about the situation were correct. Was there any topic related vocabulary which you had not predicted? What was it?

**C** **2.2** Listen to three more introductions. After each introduction, imagine the situation and language you may hear in the main dialogue. Discuss your ideas with your partner.

**D** **2.3** Listen to each dialogue. Were your predictions correct?

## 3 Identifying the question

Notes and form completion tasks don't include actual questions. Before you answer, you need to think what sort of information is required in each gap. You need to identify the question you are being asked. In the exam, you don't need to write the question down, just think about it.

**A** Complete the sentences in the first column so they are true for you. Use no more than three words and/or a number for each answer.

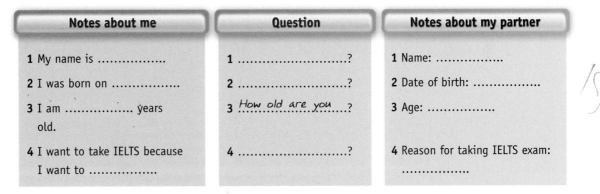

| Notes about me | Question | Notes about my partner |
|---|---|---|
| **1** My name is ................ | **1** ...........................? | **1** Name: ................ |
| **2** I was born on ................ | **2** ...........................? | **2** Date of birth: ................ |
| **3** I am ................ years old. | **3** *How old are you* ...? | **3** Age: ................ |
| **4** I want to take IELTS because I want to ................ | **4** ...........................? | **4** Reason for taking IELTS exam: ................ |

**B** Each statement in the first column is the answer to a question. For example, the third statement, 'I am ... years old', answers the question 'How old are you'. In the middle column, write questions for the other three statements.

**C** Now ask your partner questions 1–4. Complete the notes with information about your partner.

## 4 Identifying the answer type

**A** Look at the notes below. The first column contains examples of notes completion questions that might appear in the exam. What do you think the topic of the conversation will be? Discuss with a partner.

| Notes | Question word | Answer type |
|---|---|---|
| Birthday present for **1** ............ | who | name |
| Cost of sending a text: **2** ........... | | N.G...... |
| Cheapest network: **3** .......... | | |
| Cheapest time of day: **4** .......... | | |
| Can buy top-up cards at **5** .......... | | |
| Operates in over **6** .......... countries | | |
| **7** ..........% of country covered by network | | |
| Need hands-free when cycling because it's **8** .......... | | |

**B** What kinds of questions do you need to answer to complete the notes? For each gap, choose the appropriate question word from the box below and write it in the table. The first one has been done as an example.

| | | | |
|---|---|---|---|
| how many | ~~who~~ | where | what percentage |
| when | how much | why | which |

**C** Different types of question require different types of answer. For example, the answer to a 'who' question is a name. For each of the questions above, choose an answer type from the box below and write it in the table. The first one has been done as an example.

| | | | |
|---|---|---|---|
| amount of money | year | ~~name~~ | number |
| place | name | percentage | reason |

**D** 2.4 Now listen to the recording and answer questions 1–8 in the table above. Write no more than three words and/or a number for each answer.

## 5 | Form completion

### *for this task*

Form completion and notes completion tasks ask you to fill in gaps using information taken *directly* from the recording you hear.

▸ Read the instructions carefully to see how many words you are allowed to use. Remember that if you write too many words, or if you write down different words from the ones you hear, your answer will be marked as incorrect. If you spell a word incorrectly, your answer will be marked as incorrect.

▸ In the exam, there is time to look at the questions before you start listening. Use this time to read through the instructions and questions and imagine the situation. Look at each gap and identify the question and answer type.

▸ While you are listening, write down your answers because you will only hear the recording once.

▸ The questions follow the order of the recording.

 **2.5** *Questions 1–6*

*Listen to a man buying a computer and complete the notes below. Write **NO MORE THAN THREE WORDS AND/OR A NUMBER** for each answer.*

---

**Application for extended warranty on new computer**

Name: Jonathan **1** ...........................    Title: Mr / Mrs / Ms / Miss / (Dr) / Other

Address: **2** ...........................    Postcode: **3** ...........................
  Newtown

Telephone No: **4** ...........................    email address: **5** ............... @fastnet.com

Add to mailing list ? **6** ...........................

---

### *express tip*

Spelling is very important in the Listening test. When you finish each section, you must always check that each answer is spelled correctly.

## 6 | Notes completion

**2.6** *Questions 1–10*

*Listen to a customer enquiring about different types of radios and complete the notes below. Write **NO MORE THAN THREE WORDS AND/OR A NUMBER** for each answer.*

---

Model: Club Tropicana    Colour:         pink, orange and **1** ...........
                         Extra features: CD player, **2** ..........., alarm
                         No. of speakers: **3** ...........
                         Price:          **4** $ ...........

Model: Night Owl         Extra features: clock, **5** ..........., reading light
                         Battery life:   **6** ........... hours
                         Maker's name:   **7** ...........

Model: **8** ...........    Colour:         gold
                         Extra features: neck strap, free headphones
                                         uses **9** ........... power
                         Price:          **10** $ ...........

---

**2**

> **Exam task** ▶ Describing bar charts, pie charts and tables
>
> **Exam focus** ▶ Academic Writing Task 1 ▶ For General Training Task 1, go to page 72.
>
> **Skills** ▶ Understanding charts and tables; describing general and specific information; comparing and contrasting data

## 1 Introduction

Discuss these questions with a partner.

- Have you ever bought anything over the Internet? If yes, what did you buy?
- What kinds of things would you order through the Internet? Why?
- Is there anything that you wouldn't buy online? Why do you think that some people are nervous about buying things online?
- Which age group do you think makes the most purchases online?

## 2 Understanding charts and tables

**A** Before you begin writing, it is important to understand the information shown in the chart. Look at the bar chart on page 21 and discuss questions 1–4 with a partner.

1 What does the title tell you?
2 What does the vertical axis show?
3 What does the horizontal axis show?
4 What does the colour key on the right tell you?

## IN THE EXAM

### Writing module: Academic Task 1

*If you are preparing for the General Training module, turn to Unit GT 1A on page 72.*

The IELTS Writing module takes 60 minutes and consists of two tasks.

In Task 1 of the Academic Writing module, you are asked to write a report for a university lecturer in which you describe information presented visually, for example in diagrams, bar charts, pie charts or tables. Alternatively, you may be asked

to describe a process, how an object works or a sequence of events. You are expected to use a formal academic style.

You must write at least 150 words and you are assessed on the following:

- Task achievement: how well you answer the question
- Coherence and cohesion: how well your answer is organised, including how the information is linked together
- Lexical resource: the vocabulary you use
- Grammatical range and accuracy

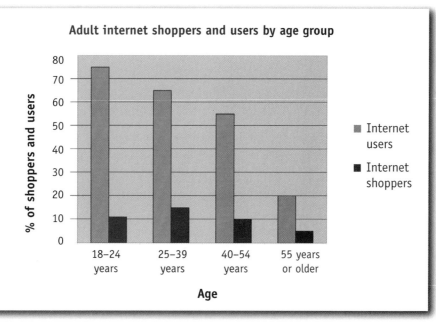

Adult internet shoppers and users by age group

**B** The information in a bar chart can be presented in table form. Complete the table by copying information from the bar chart above.

| Age | 18–24 | 25–39 | 40–54 | 55+ |
|---|---|---|---|---|
| **Internet users** | 75% | **1** ......... % | 55% | **2** ......... % |
| **Internet shoppers** | 11% | 15% | 10% | **3** ......... % |

## 3 Describing general and specific information

**A** Look at the chart in 2A. Describe the chart by putting sections a–g in the correct order (1–7).

7
.... **a** A final point to note is that the number of people shopping online does not change very much between the different age groups.

1
.... **b** The chart shows how the Internet is used by different age groups. It looks at both general use and online shopping.

.... **c** Another thing which stands out in this chart is that most people use the Internet for things other than shopping.

.... **d** More specifically, this is between about 5% and 15% in all age groups. The group making the most purchases are the 25–39-year-olds, and the group making the fewest purchases are the 55-year-olds and over.

2
.... **e** One of the first things to note is that fewer older people use the Internet than younger people.

3
.... **f** For example, 75% of 18–24-year-olds use the Net, compared with only 20% of 55-year-olds and over.

.... **g** For instance, in the youngest age group nearly 80% of people use the Internet, whereas only 10% make purchases online, although it should be noted that this difference is not as dramatic in all age groups.

**B** When you describe visual information, you should start with a general overview statement about what the chart or table shows. Then, you should choose two or three main features and describe them. Each time you pick out a main feature, use some specific detail to support it.

Read sentences 1–5 and categorise them.

**a** Which sentences are an **overview statement** of what the graph shows?

**b** Which sentences describe an **overall trend**?

**c** Which sentences provide **specific detail** used to support a main point?

1 Fewer older people use the Internet than younger people.

2 75% of 18–24-year-olds use the Net, compared with only 20% of 55-year-olds and over.

3 Most people use the Internet for things other than shopping.

4 The chart shows how the Internet is used by different age groups; it looks at both general use and online shopping.

5 In the youngest age group, nearly 80% of people use the Internet, whereas only 10% make purchases online.

## 4 Comparing and contrasting data

You can contrast information using *but, however, while, on the other hand, in/by comparison* and *in contrast*. You can add more information using *and, also, as well as, in addition, furthermore* and *not only ... but also*.

**A** Complete sentences 1–4 by choosing the correct word. There may be more than one possible answer.

1 *Although/However/While* 75% of 18–24-year-olds use the Internet, only 10% make purchases online.

2 *Although/However/While*, only 10% make purchases online.

3 *As well as/Not only* showing general internet use, *it also/but also* shows online shopping.

4 It shows *as well as/not only* general internet use, *it also/but also* online shopping.

**B** Information may also be presented as a pie chart. The pie chart below shows how one university student spent his money on internet purchases last year. Look at the information in the pie chart and choose the appropriate word(s) to make correct sentences.

1 He spent *more/less* money on airline tickets than music.

2 A *very large/relatively small* percentage of his money was spent on entertainment tickets.

3 His *biggest/smallest* expense was airline tickets.

4 He didn't spend as much money on *computer software/music* as *computer software/music*.

5 He spent much more on *airline/entertainment* tickets than on *airline/entertainment* tickets.

6 He spent *slightly/much* more on music than on books and magazines.

7 He spent *a great deal/a little* on airline tickets.

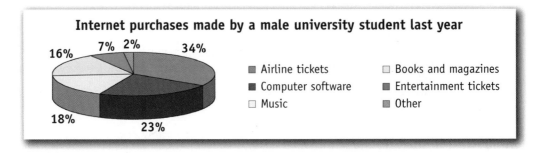

**Internet purchases made by a male university student last year**

16% 7% 2% 34%
18% 23%

■ Airline tickets  □ Books and magazines
■ Computer software  ■ Entertainment tickets
□ Music  ■ Other

**C** Write your own comparative sentences to describe the data in the charts in 2A and 4B. Include wrong information in some of your sentences and then show them to your partner. Ask your partner to identify and correct the mistakes.

## 5 Academic Writing Task 1: Report

*for this task*

▸ Spend one or two minutes studying the chart until you understand what it is showing.

▸ Explain what the chart is describing in your opening sentence.

▸ Then identify two or three main features. Don't describe everything you see. Look for any interesting features, especially surprising or contrasting information.

▸ Start with an overall description and then move on to use details to support your main points. Remember to use expressions such as *in addition* and *however* to link your ideas.

▸ Remember to leave time to check your work before the end.

You should spend about 20 minutes on this task.

*The chart below shows the different types of goods and services purchased online in Australia, Canada and the United Kingdom last year.*

*Summarise the information by selecting and reporting the main features, and make comparisons where relevant.*

Write at least 150 words.

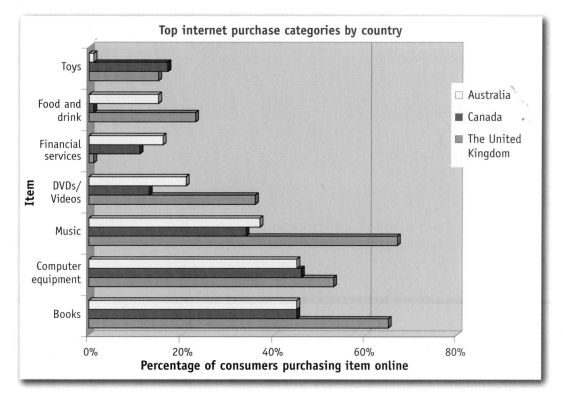

# 3 Jobs and Job-hunting

▶ **Exam tasks** ▶ Matching information to sections of text; table completion; sentence completion
▶ **Skill** ▶ Identifying keywords and paraphrase

## 1 Introduction

**A** Discuss these questions with a partner.
   • Are you working at the moment?
   • What jobs have you done in the past?
   • What is your ideal job?

**B** Work in pairs.
   **Student A:** Think of a job, but don't tell student B what it is. Answer student B's questions with 'yes' or 'no'.
   **Student B:** Try to guess your partner's job by asking 'yes/no' questions. For example: Do you work outdoors? Do you earn a lot of money? Do you wear any special clothing or a uniform?
   When student B has guessed the job, change roles.

## 2 Identifying keywords and paraphrase

In the Reading module, you are often tested on your ability to find factual information within a text. You may have to match information with a picture or sentence.

### IN THE EXAM

**Reading module: Matching information to sections of text**

In the Reading module, you may be asked to match information to sections of text. In the Academic Training module, these sections will be paragraphs from a single passage.

In the General Training module, you might have a selection of advertisements rather than a single passage. In this case, you might be asked to match pictures to advertisements or match statements to advertisements.

**A** Skim the classified advertisement below. Which of the pictures on page 24 does it refer to? Show your partner.

**Wire**

INTERNATIONAL

**£45,000 p.a.**

This market-leading news channel requires a dynamic and experienced journalist to join our team covering events in South America.

**Based in Buenos Aires, you will:**
• be fluent in Spanish and English.
• have a minimum of 3 years experience in business or marketing journalism.
• have a degree in business or marketing.
• have the initiative required to work independently.

Please email your CV to:
diane.roberts@wireinternational.com
or call Diane Roberts for more details on 020 9425 6954

**B** Read the advertisement carefully. Underline the keywords that helped you match the advertisement with the picture.

**C** Read the advertisement above and find synonyms and paraphrases (different words with the same or similar meaning) for:
1 having worked in this field before
2 being able to make decisions yourself
3 speaking other languages

## 3 Matching information to sections of text

This task consists of two parts. For *Questions 1–4,* you need to match pictures with advertisements. For *Questions 5–10,* you need to match advertisements with statements.

### for this task

| Questions 1–4 | Questions 5–10 |
|---|---|
| ▶ Try to think of different words to describe what's in each picture. Then look for keywords in the advertisements. | ▶ Look for keywords in the statements. Then look for synonyms or paraphrases of these keywords in the advertisements. |
| ▶ Match the ones you are sure about first, and then the more difficult ones second. If you can't find the answer, guess. | ▶ If a statement refers to more than one advertisement, make sure that the statement you choose matches precisely what the advertisement says. |

**Questions 1–4**

*Look at pictures 1–4 and advertisements A–D below. Match each picture with the advertisement it applies to. Write the correct letter (A–D) in the box next to the picture.*

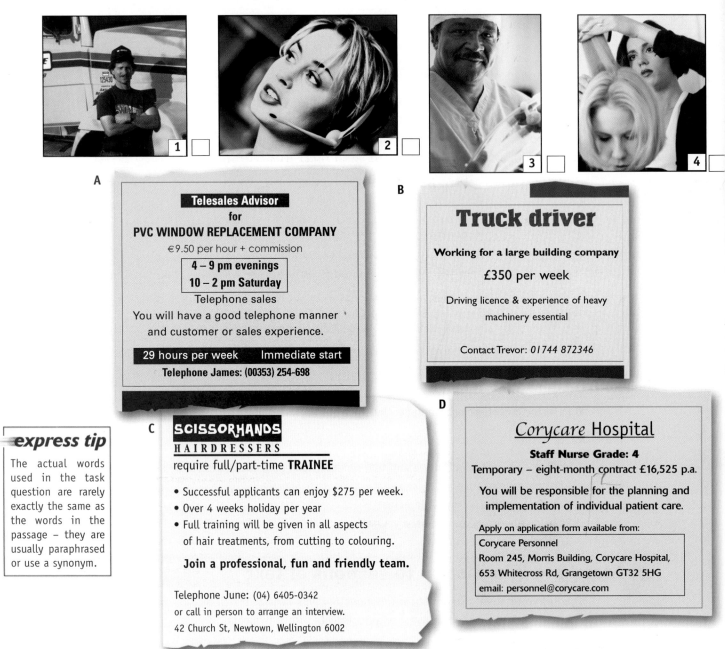

**A**

### Telesales Advisor
**for**
**PVC WINDOW REPLACEMENT COMPANY**

€9.50 per hour + commission

| **4 – 9 pm evenings** |
| **10 – 2 pm Saturday** |

Telephone sales

You will have a good telephone manner and customer or sales experience.

| 29 hours per week | Immediate start |

**Telephone James: (00353) 254-698**

**B**

# Truck driver

**Working for a large building company**

**£350 per week**

Driving licence & experience of heavy machinery essential

Contact Trevor: *01744 872346*

**C**

### SCISSORHANDS
**HAIRDRESSERS**
require full/part-time **TRAINEE**

- Successful applicants can enjoy $275 per week.
- Over 4 weeks holiday per year
- Full training will be given in all aspects of hair treatments, from cutting to colouring.

**Join a professional, fun and friendly team.**

Telephone June: (04) 6405-0342
or call in person to arrange an interview.
42 Church St, Newtown, Wellington 6002

**D**

## *Corycare* Hospital

**Staff Nurse Grade: 4**
Temporary – eight-month contract £16,525 p.a.

**You will be responsible for the planning and implementation of individual patient care.**

Apply on application form available from:

Corycare Personnel
Room 245, Morris Building, Corycare Hospital,
653 Whitecross Rd, Grangetown GT32 5HG
email: personnel@corycare.com

> **express tip**
>
> The actual words used in the task question are rarely exactly the same as the words in the passage – they are usually paraphrased or use a synonym.

**Questions 5–10**

*Look at statements 5–10 and advertisements A–D. Match each statement with the advertisement it applies to. Write the correct letter (A–D) next to each statement.*

5 You will learn how to do the job. ............
6 The position is not permanent. ............
7 You will work at the weekend. ............
8 You cannot apply by phone. ............
9 You will sell something. ............
10 You can start this job straightaway. ............

## 4 Table completion

### for this task

▸ Read the instructions carefully to see how many words and numbers you can use to answer each question.

▸ First, study the whole table. What does it tell you? For example, what are the row and column headings? These headings will tell you what kind of information is missing from the table.

▸ Then, for each gap, find the part of the text that it relates to, search that part of the text for the missing information and transfer the information to the table.

▸ In this task you are often tested on your knowledge of synonyms and paraphrases. For example, *Question 11* asks if experience is 'necessary' for each of the jobs. In the text, it says that experience is 'essential'.

**Questions 11–15**

*Complete the table below using* **NO MORE THAN THREE WORDS OR A NUMBER** *for each answer.*

---

**express tip**

In completion tasks, the questions follow the same order as the relevant information in the text.

| Job | Pay | Experience necessary | How to apply |
|---|---|---|---|
| Telesales advisor | €9.50 per hour | Yes | Telephone |
| Truck driver | £350 per week | 11 ................... | Telephone |
| Trainee hairdresser | 12 $............. per week | No | Telephone or 13 ................. |
| Nurse | 14 £............. p.a. | | Post or 15 ................. |

## 5 Sentence completion

Read the article on page 28 and answer *Questions 1–8*.

### for this task

There are two kinds of sentence completion tasks. You may be asked to complete a sentence by taking words directly from the text (*Questions 1–4*) or choosing from a list of options (*Questions 5–8*).

▸ Read each sentence and identify the section in the text it refers to.

▸ In sentence completion tasks with words from the text (*Questions 1–4*), try to predict the type of answer you are looking for. Skim the section you have identified and look for synonyms and paraphrases.

▸ In sentence completion with choices from text (*Questions 5–10*), read the options (endings) carefully. It is likely that more than one ending could complete the sentence. Read the endings again and decide which one matches exactly what the text says.

▸ Note that in sentence completion tasks questions occur in the same order as they appear in the text. The answer to *Question 7*, for example, will occur before the answer to *Question 8* in the text.

**Questions 1–4**

*Complete the sentences below with words taken from the reading passage. Write* **NO MORE THAN THREE WORDS** *for each answer.*

1 In order to make a ... you should research your choices well.  *[handwritten: better informed decision]*

2 You shouldn't choose a job simply because it has ... *[handwritten: a good salary]*

3 You might think about doing ... in order to get experience. *[handwritten: voluntary work]*

4 You can write to companies without having seen ... *[handwritten: a job advertisement]*

 **Questions 5–8**

*Complete each sentence with the correct ending A–H from the box below. Write the correct letter A–H next to sentences 5–8.*

*Para 1*

*Where do you look? Para 1 / Para 2 / Para 3*

**5** Whilst at school, you should use .........E.........

**6** The school careers officer and library will help you choose .........C.........

**7** Continuing your education will give you .........A.........

**8** You should think about the salary and .........H.........

---

**A** a bigger choice of jobs you can apply for.

**B** extra benefits.

**C** a suitable job.

**D** your CV.

**E** their facilities.

**F** further education.

**G** jobs advertised in the newspaper or job centre.

**H** your skills and interests.

---

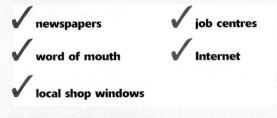

# Job-hunting:
## HOW TO BAG THAT FIRST JOB

### START LOOKING EARLY

According to the old proverb, the early bird catches the worm, and this is certainly true when it comes to deciding your future. You will get off to the best start with your job-hunting if you think about it while you are still at school. Does your school have a careers officer or library? If so, you should take advantage of them, as this will give you an idea of what's on offer and help you decide what job will suit you. Remember! Finding out as much as possible will help you make a better-informed decision.

### CONSIDER THE FUTURE

After you have left school, you may think about applying for *any* jobs that you are qualified to do. But think about the long term. Does this job have future prospects? Is it dead-end or does it have chances of promotion? Will you be happy doing this job in five, ten or twenty years' time? To open the door to a wider variety of jobs with longer-term prospects, consider further education or training.

### THINK ABOUT YOURSELF

*skills*

You should also take *yourself* into account. What are you good at? What are you interested in? Are you a 'people person' or happiest with your own company? Do you have a creative flair or are you adept at arithmetic? Don't just apply for a job because it has a good salary. Money is important, but what can the job offer you in terms of personal satisfaction?

### HOW TO LOOK

Be systematic in your search. First write down possible career paths, then think of the different jobs within this field. Think of the skills and qualifications you need to get that first valuable job, and how you might go about getting them. Don't just limit your thinking to further study. There may be other, less immediately obvious routes, such as doing voluntary work.

### WHERE TO LOOK

Traditionally, a good source of job advertisements has been newspapers, job centres and word of mouth (friends and family can have the most useful information of all), but nowadays, any job search would not be complete without access to the Internet. Use this checklist to ensure you are exploring all possible avenues.

✓ newspapers    ✓ job centres

✓ word of mouth    ✓ Internet

✓ local shop windows

### APPLY ON SPEC

A great many jobs are found without responding to a job advertisement at all. Try writing to companies enclosing your CV.

▶ **Exam focus** ▶ Speaking Part 2: Individual long turn
▶ **Skills** ▶ Checking you understand the topic card; organising your ideas

*baldness*

## 1 Introduction

**A** We often speak for a long time without being interrupted.
Tell your partner which of the following you have done:

1 told a story to friends in a café
2 made a presentation in class or at work
3 left a long message on a telephone answering machine
4 explained a complicated situation to someone

Situations 1–4 above have one thing in common: you have to think about what you are going to say and organise your ideas.

**B** Part 2 of the Speaking exam tests your ability to speak for a longer period of time. Here is a typical topic card for Part 2 of the exam. You should try to speak about all the points on the card.

Work with a partner. First, discuss some ideas you might include when speaking about the card. Then, take turns speaking about the topic on the card. Try to talk for at least two minutes.

> **Describe a job that you, or someone you know, have done.**
> **You should say:**
> **what the job was**
> **what you had to do exactly**
> **if you would do this job in the future**
> **and explain what you liked and didn't like about it.**

**C** What did you find difficult about the task? Discuss it with your partner or your teacher.

## IN THE EXAM

### Speaking module: Part 2

In Part 2 of the Speaking exam, the examiner will ask you to speak for one or two minutes on the topic of a card that you will be given.

You have one minute to prepare to speak. During this time, you can make some notes if you want to.

You will then speak, without interruption from the examiner, for one or two minutes.

When the examiner wants you to stop talking, he or she will do so by asking you one or two follow-up questions. You should spend only a few seconds answering these.

## 2 Checking you understand the topic card

**A** If you do not understand something on the card, you can ask the examiner for clarification. You can use your English to impress the examiner – even when you do not understand.

Here, a student does not understand the word 'exactly'. Look at the notes she has made on the card and read the question she asks to check the information.

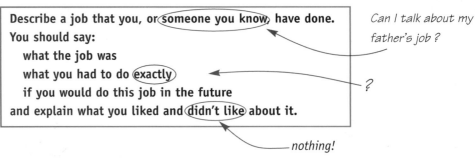

> Describe a job that you, or someone you know, have done.
> You should say:
>   what the job was
>   what you had to do exactly
>   if you would do this job in the future
> and explain what you liked and didn't like about it.

*Can I talk about my father's job?*

*?*

*nothing!*

Candidate: 'I'm sorry. Here it says "What you had to do exactly". By "exactly" do you mean what were the different things I did when I was working? For example, if I washed the dishes or served customers?'

The examiner will then either confirm the student's idea or explain the question. Useful expressions you can use include:

> By ... , do you mean ...?
> If I understand this correctly, it means that ...
> So, in other words, it's saying ...
> So, is it OK if I talk about ...?
> It says here ... but I ...

*I'm fucking guy !*

**B** Work with a partner. What other questions do you think the student asked? Practise asking questions about the card, using the expressions above.

## 3 Organising your ideas

**A** 3.1 It is important to organise your thoughts clearly and logically before you speak. Read the students' notes (A–C). The keywords have been underlined. Listen to the three students doing the exam and number the cards in the order in which you hear them. Listen for the keywords that each student wants to include.

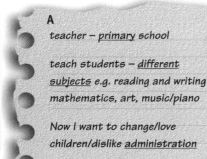

**A**

teacher – <u>primary</u> school

teach students – <u>different</u>
<u>subjects</u> e.g. reading and writing
mathematics, art, music/piano

Now I want to change/love
children/dislike <u>administration</u>

**B**

<u>Chef</u> in a hotel kitchen

make meals/40 guests
enjoyed wedding parties

Maybe, open my restaurant

<u>Creative</u> job I enjoy/very
hard work – <u>exhausted</u>

**C**

waitress – coffee bar

clean tables <u>promotion</u>
make coffee/serve customers
<u>cash register</u> for 3 months

in future? yes if student –
<u>convenient</u> + hours are <u>flexible</u>

Like – colleagues + boss
not like – <u>uniform</u>

**B** (3.1) Listen again to the students doing the test and cross off the points on their cards as they discuss them. Were there any points that they didn't cover?

**C** Look at the topic card on page 30 and make similar notes for yourself. Underline the points that you definitely want to include.

**D** Choose a different partner. Use the card to practise speaking again. This time use your notes to help you organise your thoughts.

## 4 Individual long turn

### for this task

The examiner will give you a topic card and a piece of paper and pencil to make notes.

▸ Read the card carefully. If you do not understand, ask the examiner to explain.

▸ Make some notes (in English or your own language) to help you organise your thoughts before you speak. On your notes, underline any keywords you want to make sure to include.

▸ Try to cover each point on the card but don't worry if you don't cover all the points in your notes. When talking, keep going, even if you make a mistake.

▸ Make sure to look up from your card and make eye contact with the examiner when you are speaking.

▸ Don't worry about talking for too long. The examiner will interrupt you when he or she wants you to finish. You will then be asked a few questions to end this part of the test. An example of a follow-up question that the examiner might ask you is: 'Is there any job that you would never consider doing?'

In pairs, practise the interview for two minutes.

**Student A:** You are the candidate. For one minute, look at the topic card below and make some notes to help you. Then, use your notes to speak for one or two minutes. Follow the advice in *for this task* above.

**Student B:** You are the examiner. Give Student A one minute to look at the card below and make notes. Then listen to Student A's answers carefully. Does he or she follow the advice in *for this task*? After one or two minutes, interrupt and ask Student A a few questions related to the topic.
When you have finished, change roles.

> **Describe the job that you would most like to do in the future.**
> **You should say:**
> what the job is
> what skills and qualifications you would need to get the job
> if you think you will ever do this job
> **and explain what appeals to you about this kind of work.**

# 4 Crime and Punishment

> **Exam tasks** ▶ Multiple-choice questions; short-answer questions; notes completion
> **Exam focus** ▶ Listening Section 2: Non-academic monologue; Listening Section 3: Academic dialogue
> **Skills** ▶ Using keywords to predict the answer; identifying synonyms and paraphrase

## 1 Introduction

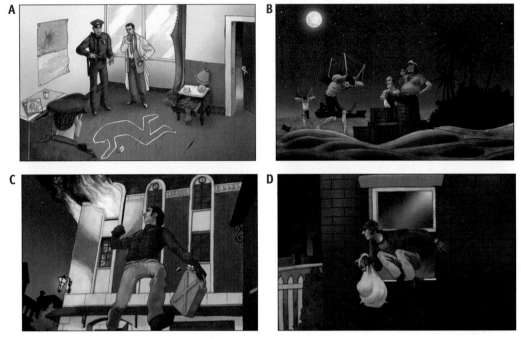

A  Work in pairs. Match pictures A–D to the crimes in the box below.

| | | | |
|---|---|---|---|
| arson | car theft | murder | robbery |
| burglary | fraud | pickpocketing | smuggling |

Four of the crimes are not illustrated. Can you define them? Do you know the names of any other crimes? Make a list.

B  Imagine you have witnessed one of the crimes in pictures A–D and are reporting it to the police. What kind of information would the police need? What questions would the police officer ask? Make a list of questions with your partner.

## IN THE EXAM

**Listening Section 2: Non-academic monologue**

Section 2 of the Listening module is a non-academic monologue. It is usually one person talking about an everyday subject, for example, holidays. However, sometimes it may feature two speakers. In this case, one of them will be speaking most of the time and the other one will be asking a few short questions.

In the exam, you will hear the recording once only.

As with Section 1, there are many different task types which may appear in this section. Two common task types are multiple-choice questions and short-answer questions.

Now  copies  Steakens

## 2 Using keywords to predict the answer

A **4.1** You will hear a businesswoman reporting the theft of her briefcase. Look at this example of a short answer question. Underline the most important words in the question. These are known as keywords.

> **1** What colour is the briefcase? ................

What kind of answer is required? Can you predict what it might be?
Now listen to the recording and answer the question.

B **4.2** Now look at question 2. Underline the keywords and try to predict the answer. Then listen to the recording and answer the question.

> **2** What important papers were in the briefcase? ..............

C **4.3** Look at this example of a multiple-choice question. What question is being asked here?

> **3** The briefcase was stolen from
> **A** the back of a car.
> **B** a dry cleaner's shop.
> **C** a dress shop.

Underline the keywords in the question stem (the first line) and the options (A, B and C).
Why is it important to underline 'dress' or 'dress shop', but not just 'shop'?
Can you predict the answer? Sometimes all answers are equally possible but it is always a good idea to think about what the answer might be before you listen. Now listen to the recording and answer the question.

## 3 Identifying synonyms and paraphrase

A **4.4** Look at this multiple-choice question and underline the keywords. Think about the question that is being asked. The recording and the question may use different words to talk about the same thing, that is, they may use synonyms or paraphrase. Before you listen, read through the options and think of different ways of expressing the same information. This way you will recognise the correct answer when you hear it. Work with a partner. Look at option A. Are there other ways of saying '12.00'? Think about what you might hear on the recording. What about '1.45' and '2.15'? Now listen to the recording and answer the question.

> *express tip*
>
> Thinking about synonyms for keywords and predicting will help you find the correct answer.

> **1** The theft occurred
> **A** around 12.00.
> **B** between 1.45 and 2.00.
> **C** between 2.00 and 2.15.

B **4.5** Look at this short-answer question and underline the keywords.

> **2** How long was the woman away from her vehicle? ...fiveman.......

Can you think of any synonyms or paraphrases for 'vehicle'?
Now listen to the recording and answer the question.

 **4.6** Look at question 3. Think about the keywords and synonyms. Then listen to the recording and answer the question.

> **3** The woman suspects her briefcase may have been stolen by
>   **A** a motorist.
>   **B** a cyclist.
>   **C** a pedestrian.

## 4 Multiple-choice questions; short-answer questions

Listen to a police officer giving information about a crime and answer *Questions 1–10*.

**for this task**

| Before you listen: | As you listen: |
|---|---|
| ▸ Read through the instructions and questions and try to imagine the situation and language. For short-answer questions, read the instructions carefully to see how many words you can use in your answer. | ▸ Listen carefully for keywords. Use the keywords to find the answer. |
| ▸ For multiple-choice questions, identify what question is being asked. For short-answer questions, identify the answer type needed. Identify keywords. Think of synonyms or paraphrases. Try to predict the answer. Try saying the possible answers to yourself. | ▸ Don't choose an option as soon as you hear it on the recording. You may hear information relating to two or more options, but only one option will be correct. |
| | ▸ If you miss a question, don't waste time thinking about it. Move on so you don't miss the next question. |
| | ▸ Remember that in short-answer questions, correct spelling is important. |

 **4.7** *Questions 1–5*

*Choose the correct letter, A, B or C.*

**1** The burglary took place at
  **A** a museum.   **B** the county hall.   **C** a local shop.

**2** The burglary took place
  **A** on Sunday night.   **B** on Thursday evening.   **C** at the weekend.

**3** The clock is
  **A** one of a pair.   **B** very valuable.   **C** the work of an unknown clockmaker.

**4** In the painting of Sir John Foxton, he is
  **A** standing by a horse.   **B** standing by a house.   **C** riding a horse.

**5** How did the burglars get in?
  **A** Through the windows.   **B** By the front door.   **C** The police don't know.

> **express tip**
>
> In the Listening module, the answers on the recording always appear in the same order as the questions.

**4.8** *Questions 6–10*

*Answer the questions below.*

Write **NO MORE THAN THREE WORDS AND/OR A NUMBER** for each answer.

**6** Where does the witness live? *obist a musem*

**7** What woke the witness up at 3.00 am? *lod music*

**8** What colour is the suspect's beard? *wite*

**9** What colour is the van?

**10** What is the telephone number for the police hotline? *0800-666000*

# 5 Multiple-choice questions; notes completion

Listen to two students discussing the details of a presentation and answer *Questions 1–10*.

**for this task**

▶ For the multiple-choice task (*Questions 1–4*), follow the instructions in *for this task* on page 34.

▶ For the notes completion task (*Questions 5–10*), follow the instructions in *for this task* on page 19.

🎧 **4.9** *Questions 1–4*

*Choose the correct letter, **A**, **B** or **C**.*

**1** The total number of crimes in the greater London area is

   **A** going up.    **B** going down.    **C** staying about the same.

**2** The number of robberies is

   **A** going up.    **B** going down.    **C** staying about the same.

**3** The number of burglaries is

   **A** going up.    **B** going down.    **C** staying about the same.

**4** Of all reported crime, vehicle crimes account for

   **A** a quarter.    **B** a half.    **C** the majority.

🎧 **4.10** *Questions 5–10*

*Complete the notes below.*

*Write **NO MORE THAN THREE WORDS AND/OR A NUMBER** for each answer.*

**Car crime facts**

% of stolen cars never returned to owners: **5** .........

Sort of car more likely to be stolen: **6** .........

30% of all car crime happens in **7** .........

**Safety tips**

At night, park car in a **8** ......... area.

Never leave **9** ......... in the car.

Never leave any other valuables where they **10** ......... .

## IN THE EXAM

### Listening Section 3: Academic dialogue

Section 3 of the Listening module is an academic dialogue where two or more students discuss an aspect of their studies, either among themselves or with a tutor.

Questions in Section 3 can be more challenging than those in Sections 1 and 2, as they test your understanding of opinions, feelings, arguments, and so on.

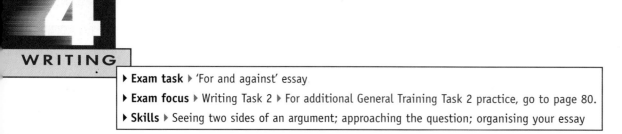

> ▸ **Exam task** ▸ 'For and against' essay
>
> ▸ **Exam focus** ▸ Writing Task 2 ▸ For additional General Training Task 2 practice, go to page 80.
>
> ▸ **Skills** ▸ Seeing two sides of an argument; approaching the question; organising your essay

## ① Introduction

**A** Do you agree or disagree with the following opinions? Circle the number that reflects your opinion.

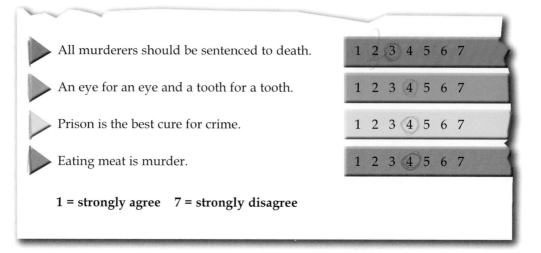

All murderers should be sentenced to death.     1 2 ③ 4 5 6 7

An eye for an eye and a tooth for a tooth.     1 2 3 ④ 5 6 7

Prison is the best cure for crime.     1 2 3 ④ 5 6 7

Eating meat is murder.     1 2 3 ④ 5 6 7

**1 = strongly agree     7 = strongly disagree**

**B** Discuss your answers with a partner. Provide reasons to support your answer.

## ② Seeing two sides of an argument

**A** In order to write good 'for and against' essays, you first need to be able to generate ideas from two opposing points of view. Look at the first opinion in 1A and identify statements 1–6 as either **for** (F) or **against** (A) the death penalty. The first one has been done as an example.

...A..  **1** Murder is wrong, whether it is committed by an individual or by the state.

...A...  **2** The death penalty is a softer option than a life sentence.

...F....  **3** Prison is expensive. Why should society have to pay?

.......  **4** Fear of the death penalty helps prevent crime.

.......  **5** Some murderers ask for the death penalty. Why should we stop them?

.......  **6** Even murderers can later regret their actions and change their ways.

> **express tip**
>
> In the exam, spend five minutes planning your essay. Draw two columns ('for' and 'against') and list three to four points for each side of the argument.

**B** Work in pairs. Think of three arguments *for* and three arguments *against* the rest of the opinions in 1A.

### IN THE EXAM

Writing Task 2 is always a discursive essay question where you are given a point of view, an argument or a problem and asked for your opinions on the question.

The essay question is very often worded 'Do you agree or disagree?' or 'To what extent do you agree or disagree?'. You can approach these questions in two ways. You can agree OR disagree (see unit 8) or you can agree AND disagree, which is known as a 'for and against' essay.

'For and against' essays look equally at both sides of the argument and do not include the writer's personal opinion until the conclusion.

For questions that ask you to discuss the advantages and disadvantages of something, you must use the 'for and against' approach.

You must write at least 250 words. Task 2 essays are assessed on the following criteria: Task response – how well you answer the question, i.e. the content and ideas. Coherence and cohesion – how your essay is organised and how the different parts are connected. Lexical resource – have you used an appropriate range of vocabulary? Grammatical range and accuracy – have you used a range of grammatical structures and have these been used accurately?

## 3 Approaching the question

**A** Read the sample exam question below. With a partner, ask and answer the brainstorming questions for each of the keywords.

> **express tip**
> Asking yourself questions about each of the key words in the essay question will help you to plan your answer.

What is meant by a 'cure for crime'? Why might prison not be a 'cure for crime'?

What is the purpose of prison?

What are typical prison sentences in your country? Why might it be a good idea to reduce prison sentences?

**Prison** is not a **cure for crime.**

To reduce crime in the long-term, courts should significantly **reduce prison sentences** and focus on **education** and **community work** to help criminals not to **re-offend**.

To what extent do you agree or disagree with this opinion?

What should criminals learn about in prison?

Why might prisoners commit crimes again? How can we stop prisoners from re-offending?

What type of community work is suitable for criminals? Should all criminals be able to do community work?

**B** Your essay should include views for and against the statement in the exam question, like two people having an argument. Read the arguments presented by Ms For. Then match arguments 1–4 with keywords a–d.

**a** education **b** re-offend **c** reduce sentences **d** community work

**1** 'In prison, people find out how to commit crimes from other prisoners, and may use that knowledge when they are released.'

**2** 'Helping old people, cleaning the streets, etc. is useful for society.'

**3** 'People need to learn skills inside prison so they can be prepared for the outside world.'

**4** 'Prisons are overcrowded and expensive. If we cut prison sentences, we can cut overcrowding and save money.'

**C** With a partner, think of what Mr Against might say to counter each of these four arguments.

## 4 Organising your essay

**A** Read the model student essay below based on the sample exam question in 3A. The essay is divided into four sections: introduction, first half of main body, second half of main body and conclusion. Each section is represented by a separate paragraph (A–D). What is the function of each paragraph? Label the paragraphs 1–4.

**1** It lists and supports the arguments against the question.

**2** It summarises the arguments for and against the question and states your personal opinion.

**3** It presents the question again to show clearly that there is an argument with two sides.

**4** It lists and supports the arguments in favour of the question.

**A** **There are many different opinions on [a]** the best way to reduce crime. The traditional solution is to be hard on criminals and put them in prison for a very long time. **An opposing view [b]** is expressed by people with more modern ideas. **They think that [c]** education and community work are the long-term solutions to cutting crime. So who is right – the traditionalists or the modernists?

.............

**B** **People in favour of [d]** reducing prison sentences often argue that prisons should not simply be places of punishment. In traditional prisons, people learn a lot about crime, **so [e]** when they leave prison, they will commit more crimes. Education, **however [f]**, gives people the skills to get a job when they leave prison, **which means that [g]** they will probably not re-offend. Part-time work experience in the community is also very helpful **as [h]** it is a step back into everyday life in society. People can be in prison, but they can also feel they are doing useful work.

.............

**C** **On the other hand [i]**, **some people argue that [j]** long prison sentences are right **because [k]** the punishment should fit the crime. If, **for example [l]**, someone commits a serious crime **such as [m]** bank robbery, they should go to prison for a long time. **They also believe that [n]** reducing prison sentences significantly reduces people's fear of prison and **consequently [o]**, people will commit more crimes. People will not be frightened of going to a prison which is like a university with learning and work experience opportunities.

.............

**D** **In short [p]**, **I agree that [q]** education and community work can have an important role in helping reduce crime, **but [r]** there should be strict controls on the type of community work prisoners can do. **It is important to understand that [s]** some people are a real danger to society and need to stay in prison for a very long time.

.............

**B** Look at the useful language structures in bold. Read the essay again and find an example for each of the functions (1–7) below. There may be more than one example for each of the functions.

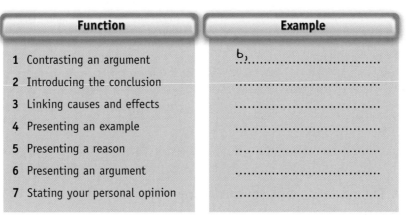

| Function | Example |
|---|---|
| 1 Contrasting an argument | b) ........................... |
| 2 Introducing the conclusion | ........................... |
| 3 Linking causes and effects | ........................... |
| 4 Presenting an example | ........................... |
| 5 Presenting a reason | ........................... |
| 6 Presenting an argument | ........................... |
| 7 Stating your personal opinion | ........................... |

**C** Complete the following sentences using your own ideas.

1 The number of police officers on our streets has increased over the last few years. However,

................................................................................................................

2 People are more worried about crime now because

................................................................................................................

3 There are many alternatives to prison, such as

................................................................................................................

4 These days, the police spend a lot of their time doing paperwork, which means that

................................................................................................................

## 5 Academic and General Training: Essay

### for this task

▶ When you take a two-sided, 'for and against' approach to an essay, you should present both sides of an argument, even if you personally agree with only one of them.

▶ Identify the keywords in the question and brainstorm arguments for and against the viewpoint you need to discuss. Decide which of these arguments you will include in the essay.

▶ Decide how you will structure your essay. You may, for example, use a four-paragraph approach (see page 38) to organise your essay.

▶ Connect and support your arguments using language structures, such as *for example ..., which means that ..., consequently ..., however ...,* etc.

▶ Allow a few minutes at the end to check your essay for spelling, punctuation and grammar mistakes.

You should spend about 40 minutes on this task.

Write about the following topic:

*In order to reduce crime, we need to attack the causes of crime such as poverty and lack of educational opportunities. It is not enough to simply have more police on the street and put more people into prison.*

*To what extent do you agree or disagree with this opinion?*

Give reasons for your answer and include any relevant examples from your own knowledge or experience.

Write at least 250 words.

# 5 Transport and Inventions

▸ **Exam tasks** ▸ Matching headings to paragraphs; multiple-choice questions
▸ **Skills** ▸ Building a mental map of the text; rebuilding the text

## 1 Introduction

Discuss these questions with a partner.

• Have you ever flown in a plane? Do you like flying? Why/Why not?
• Apart from aeroplanes, what other ways of flying are there?

## 2 Building a mental map of the text

**A** Reading a text can be like going to a new city – it can be difficult to find your way around. A useful technique to help you navigate a text is to build a map of the passage, in your mind, as you are reading. When you read the first paragraph, you can see how the rest of the passage will develop. Paragraphs 1–4 are first paragraphs from different texts and tell us something about the development of the text they are taken from. Read them and then match them with the types of text maps (i–iv).

**1**

For thousands of years, humans have looked at the skies and dreamed of flying. Early attempts to fly, using wings made from feathers, were unsuccessful and in many cases ended in disaster. The use of hot air and light gases eventually allowed humans to reach for the skies, but it was not until the early 1900s that gliders and then powered planes fully realised man's dream to fly.

**2**

**How a road is built: Fact sheet**

The following steps outline the stages involved in road building, some of which occur concurrently.
First of all, it is necessary

### IN THE EXAM

**Academic and General Training: Reading passages**

While the task types of the Academic and General Reading modules are the same, the types of reading passages differ. The Academic module will usually contain at least one passage organised as a logical argument, while the readings in the General Training module are likely to be more descriptive or instructive. The organisation of non-argumentative texts may vary, but common types are: categories, chronological description and describing a process.

**3**

There are many reasons put forward for not privatising public transport, especially a country's railway system. However, some people think privatisation is a good idea and it improves individual freedom, increases efficiency, makes the railway management listen to the customer more, decreases public debt and also reduces the problems created by unions. Let us look at each of these arguments in turn.

**4**

Buying a train ticket in the UK can be more than a little confusing. There are many different ticket types and prices, and it is worth doing a little research, which could save you more than 50% on the cost of your travel.

| Types of text maps | Paragraph |
|---|---|
| **i** Categories (groups of things according to type) | ................................... |
| **ii** Chronological order (time or historical order) | ................................... |
| **iii** A process (first you do this, then you do that, etc.) | ................................... |
| **iv** Building an argument (firstly, secondly, also, etc.) | ................................... |

**B** Paragraph 1 is the beginning of the passage on page 42. Read the passage and put the following inventions in historical order (1 = oldest, 7 = most modern). Because the passage follows a chronological map, the text order and the historical order should be the same.

| | | | |
|---|---|---|---|
| kites | .......... | hot air balloon | .......... |
| jet plane | .......... | wings (for birdmen) | .......... |
| glider | .......... | propeller planes | .......... |
| ornithopter | .......... | | |

## 3 Rebuilding the text

The passage 'Man's Passion for Flight' on page 42 follows a chronological map, but other passages may follow different types of maps – categories, a process or building an argument. Whichever type of map is used, it is essential to be clear about the main idea in each paragraph.

**A** Look at paragraphs A and B on page 42. Which one of the following is the main idea of each paragraph?

**Paragraph A**
1 The inventors were very clever.
2 Powered planes were the most successful.
3 Flying has a long history.

**Paragraph B**
1 Wax melts in the sun.
2 Ancient Greek legend tells of men flying using birds' wings.
3 Icarus made a mistake by flying too near to the sun.

**B** Work in pairs. Create a map of the text by thinking of headings for paragraphs C–H. Write your headings on a piece of paper.

**C** Work with a partner. Using your map and your answers from 2B, try to give an account of the passage without looking at it.

# Man's passion for flight

**A**

For thousands of years, humans have looked at the skies and dreamed of flying. Early attempts to fly, using wings made from feathers, were unsuccessful and in many cases ended in disaster. The use of hot air and light gases eventually allowed humans to reach for the skies, but it was not until the early 1900s that gliders and then powered planes fully realised man's dream to fly.

**B**

One of the earliest tales of man's passion for flight comes from Greek mythology. According to legend, an inventor named Daedalus and his son Icarus escaped from a prison on the island of Crete by making wings of wax and feathers. Daedalus was successful in returning home, but Icarus flew too near to the sun, the wax on his wings melted, the feathers came out and he fell to his death in the sea.

**C**

Around 400 BC, the first kites were created by the Chinese, who used them for religious ceremonies and also for the testing of weather conditions. In many ways, this early invention paved the way for the introduction of balloons and gliders many years later.

**D**

Perhaps the most important early aviation pioneer was the artist and inventor Leonardo da Vinci, who in the 1480s produced over one hundred sketches to illustrate how humans might be able to fly. These included a drawing of a flying machine called an *Ornithopter*. Although never created, the design for da Vinci's machine included many concepts that were later incorporated into the modern-day helicopter.

**E**

The first successful air passengers were not actually humans at all. In 1783, the Montgolfier brothers sent a duck, a sheep and a rooster up in their new invention: the hot air balloon. The flight was a success. The balloon climbed to a height of 6,000 feet and travelled more than a mile. This was soon followed by the first manned flight, which took place in Paris on 21st November 1783.

**F**

Although hot air balloons enabled people to fly freely in the air, they did not allow much control over direction. The man who first proposed an effective alternative to the balloon was George Cayley (1773–1857), who designed many different versions of gliders, including biplanes and gliders with tails. Cayley understood two important principles of flight: firstly, he was aware that air flow over the wings was crucial for producing flight, and therefore wing shape was an important factor; he also knew that any long flight would need an additional, essential ingredient – power.

**G**

In the early 1900s, two American brothers, Orville and Wilbur Wright, began to create their own version of the glider. Using the results of research carried out by Cayley and other pioneers, as well as their own experiments using wind tunnels, the brothers finally came up with a design for an engine-driven propeller system that would pull an airplane forward and create enough lift for it to fly. On 17th December 1903, at Kitty Hawk in North Carolina, the first heavier-than-air flight took place, when Orville piloted the world's first airplane, *The Flyer*. The flight covered 20 feet and lasted 12 seconds.

**H**

This first powered flight led to several important technological developments during the twentieth century, including the invention of the jet engine, large passenger planes and supersonic flight. Just over a century after the Wright Brothers' flight, a new milestone was set on 21st June 2004, when a rocket plane called *SpaceShipOne* flew to the edge of space and returned safely to Earth. None of these achievements, however, would have been possible without the efforts of the early pioneers who dared to believe that one day man's dream to fly would become a reality.

## 4 Matching headings to paragraphs

### for this task

In this type of matching task, you are given a list, from which you need to choose the best heading for each paragraph in a passage. There are always more headings than paragraphs, so you do not need to use all of them.

▶ In the exam, skim the passage quickly and build a map of the text by noting the main idea of each paragraph. For *Questions 1–8*, use the map you created in 3B.

▶ Look at the list of headings and compare it to your map of the text. Match as many headings as you can without reading the passage again, and cross off the headings you have used (including the example).

▶ Read the paragraphs you have not matched and the remaining headings again.

**Questions 1–8**

*The passage on page 42 has eight paragraphs **A–H**. Choose the correct heading for each paragraph from the list of headings below. Write the correct numbers **i–x** next to the paragraphs. The first one has been done as an example.*

> **List of Headings**
>
> i The first powered flight
> ii Pushing the limits of technology
> iii The first international flight
> iv Planes without engines
> v How a hot air balloon works
> vi Birdmen
> vii The genius who saw the future
> viii The first man-made things to fly
> ix The flying farm
> x The long history of flying

1 Paragraph A  ....**X**......
2 Paragraph B  ............
3 Paragraph C  ............
4 Paragraph D  ............

5 Paragraph E  ............
6 Paragraph F  ............
7 Paragraph G  ............
8 Paragraph H  ............

## 5 Multiple-choice questions

**A** You can use your map to help you quickly find the answer to multiple-choice questions. Look at this example.

9 According to Greek legend, Icarus never got home because

 **A** he was exhausted and fell into the sea.

 **B** the wings became too hot and he crashed.

 **C** the sun burnt him.

 **D** he was recaptured and taken to prison.

Before you consider options A, B, C or D, think about the following:

• What keywords in the question will help you identify the relevant section in the passage?

• Which paragraph do you need to look at?

**B** Here are the first parts of *Questions 10–14.* Underline the keywords. Then use your map to help you find the paragraphs in the passage which will contain the answers.

| Question | | Paragraph |
|---|---|---|
| *Question 10:* | The Chinese were very good at making | .......................... |
| *Question 11:* | Which modern flying machine is based on a 500-year-old design? | .......................... |
| *Question 12:* | The first powered flight was performed by | .......................... |
| *Questions 13–14:* | According to the information in the passage, which **TWO** factors did George Cayley realise would be necessary for a long flight? | .......................... |

**C** Now answer *Questions 10–14.*

**for this task**

In the Reading module, there are multiple-choice questions with a single answer and multiple-choice questions with multiple answers. In the first type, you are asked to choose one answer from four possible answers; in the second, you are asked to choose more than one answer from a longer list of possible answers. Multiple-choice questions always follow the order of the information in the passage.

▹ Look at the keywords in the question. Use your map to locate the answer in the passage. Read that section carefully.

▹ Look at options A–D and cross out the options that are clearly wrong.

▹ Before you select an option, make sure that it actually answers the question. The text may contain references to more than one option, but only one option will actually answer the question.

 **Questions 10–12**

*Choose the correct letter* **A–D**.

**10** The Chinese were very good at making

    **A**    weather balloons.

    **B**    sketches of flying machines.

    **C**    gliders.

    **D**    kites.

**11** Which modern flying machine is based on a 500-year-old design?

    **A**    helicopter

    **B**    plane

    **C**    hot air balloon

    **D**    kite

**12** The first powered flight was performed by

    **A**    Leonardo da Vinci.

    **B**    the Montgolfier brothers.

    **C**    George Cayley.

    **D**    Orville Wright.

 **Questions 13–14**

*Choose* **TWO** *letters* **A–E**.

According to the information in the passage, which **TWO** factors did George Cayley realise would be necessary for a long flight?

| **List of Factors** |
|---|
| **A**  Planes should be light. |
| **B**  Effective steering would make balloons more efficient. |
| **C**  Planes required an engine. |
| **D**  Tails enabled biplanes to travel further. |
| **E**  There should be airflow over the wings of a plane. |

**13** ..............

**14** ..............

> ▸ **Exam focus** ▸ Speaking Part 3: Two-way discussion
> ▸ **Skills** ▸ Identifying types of questions; giving an appropriate response; introducing and supporting an opinion

## 1 Introduction

**A** Look at this list of transport problems. Which do you think is the most serious transport problem in your country? Why? Discuss your answers with a partner.

- pollution
- traffic
- parking
- unreliable public transport
- expensive public transport
- overcrowded public transport

**B** Look at the list of solutions to transport problems below. Rank them according to how effectively you think they can resolve the transport problems in your country (1 = most effective, 7 = least effective). Discuss your answers with your partner.

- increase car tax ......................
- limit the number of cars entering the city centre ......................
- build new underground train lines ......................
- create more bus lanes on existing roads ......................
- introduce new comfortable air-conditioned buses ......................
- introduce tough environmental laws to stop car pollution ......................
- build more roads ......................

**C** Can you think of any other solutions to transport problems in your country? Make a list.

### IN THE EXAM

**Speaking Part 3: Two-way discussion**

In Part 3 of the Speaking exam, the examiner will ask you to express your opinion on topics related to the one you spoke about in Part 2.

In Part 2 of the exam, you talked about your personal experiences, while in Part 3 you will be asked to give your personal opinion on subjects which are academic and theoretical in nature.

Part 3 usually lasts about four to five minutes.

## 2 Identifying types of questions

A Create questions on the topic of transport by matching 1–4 with a–d.

| | |
|---|---|
| **1** What do you think would happen d | **a** should pay higher taxes if they have bigger cars. What do you think? |
| **2** How do you think c | **b** should spend more money on building roads or railways? |
| **3** Do you think we b | **c** transport will change in the next ten years? |
| **4** Some people say that car drivers a | **d** if cities stopped investing in public transport? |

B Part 3 questions are similar to the ones above and may ask you to compare and contrast, hypothesise, speculate or evaluate. Match questions 1–4 above with functions i–iv below. The first one has been done as an example.

| | | |
|---|---|---|
| **i** | Compare and contrast: study two or more options and talk about their differences and similarities. | ....3.... |
| **ii** | Hypothesise: talk about an imagined situation in the present or future. | ....1.... |
| **iii** | Speculate: talk about what might happen in the present or future. | ......... |
| **iv** | Evaluate: decide how much you agree or disagree by discussing the arguments. | ......... |

## 3 Giving an appropriate response

A The language you use to introduce your answer depends on the type of question you are asked. If you are asked to give a general opinion, you can use *I think ...* or *In my opinion ...* . However, if the examiner asks you to hythothesise, speculate, evaluate or compare and contrast, you can use the replies below to introduce your answer.
Complete the table with functions i–iv from 2B.

**express tip**

In order to buy time, you can use language fillers such as: *Well ...,* *Mmm ...* or *It's difficult to say, but ....*

| Function | Reply |
|---|---|
| **1** ........................ | (If + past tense) I'd imagine/I'd think/I'd expect + ... would |
| **2** ........................ | I (completely/totally/tend to/don't really) agree/disagree <br> I agree/disagree to an extent, but ... |
| **3** ........................ | It's difficult to say but maybe ... <br> I'm not sure but maybe .../Maybe/Perhaps ... |
| **4** ........................ | For me, ... is more/less important ... <br> Argument X. On the other hand, Argument Y. |

B Look at questions 1–4 in 2A again. In pairs, ask and answer questions 1 and 2. Use the language in the table above to introduce your answers.

C 5.1 *How* you say something can often be just as important as *what* you say. Listen to three students answering questions from 2A and write the order (1–3) in which each speaker talks.

| | | |
|---|---|---|
| Raj sounds interested and enthusiastic. He gives full responses to all questions. He gives informative and original answers. He varies language in giving opinions. | Li Lin gives full responses and original answers, but sounds uninterested and unenthusiastic. | Carlos gives limited answers and sounds uninterested. |

## 4 Introducing and supporting an opinion

**A** **5.2** Listen to four extracts of short conversations (1–4) between an examiner and a candidate. For each conversation, tick one box in the first column which describes the opinion expressed by the speaker.

| Opinion | Ways of expressing an opinion | Reasons to support opinion |
|---|---|---|
| 1 ☐ No cars in city centre<br>☐ Need more buses | ☐ If the government did this<br>☐ I think it'd be a good idea | ☐ Too much pollution<br>☐ Too many buses |
| 2 ☐ Spend money on roads<br>☐ Spend money on trains | ☐ For me, ... is less important<br>☐ For me, ... is more important | ☐ People prefer cars<br>☐ Example of uncomfortable trains in home country |
| 3 ☐ Speed limit is too low<br>☐ Speed limit is too high | ☐ I completely agree<br>☐ I completely disagree | ☐ Example of another country<br>☐ Too much traffic at night |
| 4 ☐ Drivers shouldn't pay higher taxes<br>☐ People should drive small cars | ☐ Perhaps<br>☐ I tend to disagree | ☐ Logical explanation why higher taxes are unfair<br>☐ Example of new cars which use less petrol |

**B** **5.2** Listen to the conversations again. For each conversation, tick the right box(es) in each column to show how the speakers express their opinion and the reasons they provide to support their opinions.

**C** In pairs, discuss the opinions above.

## 5 Two-way discussion

**for this task**

▸ Listen carefully to the examiner's question. Decide whether you are asked to speculate, hypothesise, etc. and introduce your answer with the appropriate language.

▸ Express your opinions, and support and justify your ideas. In other words, tell the examiner what you think

and why you think it. Provide examples to support your opinions.

▸ Try to sound interested, give full responses to questions and use fillers to give you extra thinking time.

▸ Use a variety of language to express your ideas – not just *I think ...* and *In my opinion ...* .

Now write more questions on the topic of transport, using the ideas in the box below. For example: 'Do you think the government should stop people using mobile phones while driving?'

| | |
|---|---|
| mobile phones and driving | improve road safety |
| seatbelts in back of car | causes of car accidents |

In pairs, practise the two-way discussion using your list of questions.

**Student A:** Ask your partner questions from your list. Don't forget to ask follow-up questions for each one.

**Student B:** Listen to your partner's questions and give full, detailed responses. Be sure to give examples and reasons to support your arguments and opinions.

# 6

**LISTENING**

# The Natural World

▸ **Exam tasks** ▸ Classification; table completion; summary completion
▸ **Exam focus** ▸ Listening Section 3: Academic dialogue
▸ **Skills** ▸ Identifying attitude; identifying speakers

## 1 Introduction

**A Everything man touches he destroys.**

*J. Krishnamurti (1895–1986)*

What does Krishnamurti mean?

**B** Do you agree or disagree with Krishnamurti? Discuss your opinion with a partner.

## 2 Identifying attitude

**A 6.1** Look at opinions a–d. Listen to these four opinions and number them in the order in which you hear them. The first one has been done as an example.

| | | Opinions | | Responses |
|---|---|---|---|---|
| .......... | **a** | It is the responsibility of the government, not the individual, to protect the environment. | **i** | I'm not sure I follow you … |
| .......... | **b** | It is unacceptable to experiment on animals. | **ii** | Absolutely … |
| .......... | **c** | People should only consume food that is grown locally and naturally occurs in a particular season. | **iii** | You can't be serious! |
| ....1..... | **d** | It is wrong to keep animals in cages. | **iv** | Yeah, but … |

---

## IN THE EXAM

### Listening Section 3: Academic dialogue

Section 3 of the Listening module is an academic dialogue. It usually involves an academic discussion between two or three people. Many different task types may occur in this section, but you are often required to identify the speakers' attitude or opinion and/or identify who the speakers are. Matching and classification tasks are common in Section 3.

In matching tasks, you are asked to match questions to a list of possible answers. There are usually more possible answers than questions and you can use each answer only once.

In classification tasks, you are given a list of possible answers. You will probably use all the answers and you may use each answer more than once.

**B** **6.2** Listen again and match opinions a–d with responses i–iv.

**C** What is the attitude of the speaker of each response? Match attitudes 1–4 with responses i–iv.

**1** disagreement ......      **2** confusion ......      **3** agreement ......      **4** disbelief ......

**D** Different people will have different attitudes to the same statement, and each attitude may be expressed in different ways. Work in small groups. Can you think of different ways to express the attitudes in the table below?

| Agreement | Disagreement | Interest | Confusion | Disbelief |
|---|---|---|---|---|
| I agree ... | I don't think so ... | Really! | Sorry. I don't understand ... | You can't be serious! |

**E** In your groups, discuss opinions a–d in 2A using the expressions in the table above.

## 3 Identifying speakers

**A** **6.3** Classification and matching tasks where you need to match speakers to statements can be challenging because there are often three speakers. Listen to a conversation with three speakers discussing zoos and tick the box below each speaker's name every time he or she speaks. How many times does Cedric speak? ......

| Amina | Dr Bannister | Cedric |
|---|---|---|
|  |  |  |

**B** **6.3** Listen to the conversation again. Write the correct letter A–C next to questions 1–4.

| **A** Amina | **B** Dr Bannister | **C** Cedric |
|---|---|---|

1 Who enjoys zoos a lot?                                    .........
2 Who used to sponsor an animal?                            .........
3 Who talks about the destruction of natural habitats?      .........
4 Who is upset seeing animals in small cages?               .........

---

**express tip**

As you listen to the dialogue, point to the speaker's name and tell yourself who is speaking, like a football commentator describing who has the ball.

## 4 Classification

### for this task

In classification tasks, you are given a list of possible answers to a range of questions. You will probably use all the answers and you may use each answer more than once. In this case, the three possible answers are the names of the speakers in the conversation.

**Before you listen**

▶ Read the instructions and questions carefully.

▶ Identify the keywords in the questions and think about

synonyms or paraphrases you might hear on the recording.

**As you listen**

▶ Keep track of who is talking and listen out for keywords.

▶ Write down the answers as you listen. Remember, you don't have to write the names of the speakers, just the corresponding letter.

 **6.4** *Questions 1–7*

*You will hear some students responding to a survey on vivisection.*
*Write the correct letter, **A**, **B** or **C** next to questions 1–7.*

**A** Dawn
**B** Eddie
**C** Fran

**1** Who has been ill? .............................
**2** Who is conducting a survey? .............................
**3** Who supports vivisection? .............................
**4** Who thinks animals should have rights? .............................
**5** Who talks about advances made through research? .............................
**6** Who thinks testing cosmetics on animals is unnecessary? .............................
**7** Who talks about using computer simulation for research? .............................

## 5 Table completion; summary completion

### for this task

Table and summary completion tasks ask you to fill in gaps in the questions using information from the recording. These tasks should be approached in a similar way to form completion or notes completion tasks.

**Before you listen**

▶ Read the instructions carefully to see how many words you can use in your answer.

▶ In table completion tasks, look at the column and row headings to determine what kind of information is required in each gap. Identify how the questions are numbered: left to right or up and down.

▶ In summary completion tasks, read through the summary to get a general understanding.

▶ For each gap in the summary, identify the answer type needed. Then identify the keywords in the surrounding sentence and think of any synonyms or paraphrases you might hear on the recording.

**As you listen**

▶ Write your answers as you listen.

▶ Remember that you must use the exact words that you hear on the recording. If you write different words, your answer will be marked as incorrect.

 **6.5** A *Questions 1–12*

*You will hear two students giving a talk on 'big cats'.*
*Complete the table below. Write **NO MORE THAN THREE WORDS AND/OR A NUMBER** for each answer.*

| | Status | Weight of adult | Found in | Hunting behaviour | Prey includes | Additional notes |
|---|---|---|---|---|---|---|
| lion | not endangered | 160 – **1** ........... kg (male) | plains in **2** ........... | females do most of work; usually hunt in teams of **3** ........... | gazelle, **4** ..........., wildebeest, buffalo | **5** ........... share responsibility for rearing cubs in pride |
| cheetah | endangered and **6** .......... | 30–50 kg | Africa, Middle East, South Central Asia | usually alone, sometimes **7** .......... to bring down larger prey | springbok, warthog, gazelle | can reach speeds of **8** .......... kph |
| ocelot | threatened with extinction | **9** .......... kg | Southern US, Central and South America (but not in **10** ..........) | hunt alone, usually in **11** .......... | rodents, reptiles, fish | catch fish by flipping them out of water with **12** .......... and pouncing on them |

**6.6** B *Questions 1–6*

*You will hear two students discussing an Environmental Studies lecture.*
*Complete the summary below. Write* **NO MORE THAN THREE WORDS** *for each answer.*

---

# Factors influencing river life

A river's speed determines which species of plants and animals can live in it. Normally, the faster the river flows, the more **1** ......... it contains. But fast-flowing water is more difficult for some species to swim in.

A river may pass over several types of rock. Each rock type influences both the water and the species of **2** ......... it can support. For example, the freshwater crayfish needs lots of oxygen and lime to build up its thick outer skeleton; a fast-flowing river going over chalk is ideal.

Man also influences river life. Some rivers are used by large **3** ......... boats and have to be dredged deeply to maintain a deep channel, preventing natural development of the river bottom. Smaller boats require the removal of water plants, reducing habitat for wildlife. The wash from fast motor boats erodes the river banks, flooding animals' **4** ......... and washing away wildlife.

Finally, **5** ......... has a great effect on river life. The most common types are: sewage, **6** ......... and other waste from industry, oil, pesticides and fertilisers, litter, detergents, large amounts of hot water, animal waste and dense or decaying plant growth.

---

## express tip

In all listening sections, spelling is very important. If you misspell a word, your answer will be marked as incorrect.

# 6 WRITING

> **Exam task** ▸ Describing trends in line graphs and tables
> **Exam focus** ▸ Academic Writing Task 1 ▸ For General Training Task 1, go to page 76.
> **Skills** ▸ Using the language of trends; describing trends

## 1 Introduction

**A 1** Match the three cities in the table below with the photos above.
What do you think the weather is like in each place?

**2** What is the weather like in different parts of your country? How does it change throughout the year?

**B** Study the table and line graph below and answer the following questions.

**1** What do the table and line graph show?

**2** How are rainfall and temperature measured?

**3** Which city has the highest/lowest temperature in a year?

**4** Which city is the driest/wettest on average?

**Average monthly rainfall (mm)**

|  | J | F | M | A | M | J | J | A | S | O | N | D |
|---|---|---|---|---|---|---|---|---|---|---|---|---|
| Singapore | 252 | 173 | 193 | 188 | 173 | 173 | 170 | 196 | 178 | 208 | 254 | 257 |
| Cairo | 5 | 5 | 5 | 3 | 3 | 0–3 | 0 | 0 | 0–3 | 0–3 | 3 | 5 |
| New Delhi | 23 | 18 | 13 | 8 | 13 | 74 | 180 | 172 | 117 | 10 | 3 | 10 |

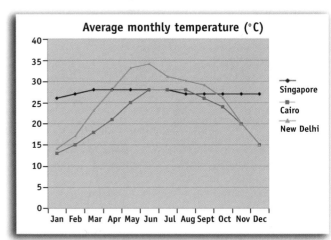

Average monthly temperature (°C)

## IN THE EXAM

### Writing module: Academic Task 1

*If you are preparing for the General Training module, turn to Unit GT 1B on page 76.*

In Task 1 of the Academic module, you are presented with visual information, which is often in the form of a graph. You are asked to describe it in a short report for a university lecturer using your own words.

Sometimes, you are asked to describe a single graph; other times you are asked to describe (and compare) more than one graph.

You must write a minimum of 150 words. As you receive only one third of your marks for Task 1, spend no more than one third of your time on this section of the writing exam – 20 minutes.

## 2 Using the language of trends

**A** To describe the information in line graphs, tables and bar charts, you need to be familiar with the vocabulary used to describe trends. Match each arrow symbol with the correct verbs and verb phrases, and nouns and noun phrases in the table below.

| Direction of trend | Verbs and verb phrases | Nouns and noun phrases |
|---|---|---|
| 1 | remain stable, remain constant, level off | no change, a levelling off |
| 2 | fluctuate, move up and down | a fluctuation |
| 3 | fall to a low point | a low point, a low |
| 4 | reach a peak, reach a high | a peak, a high |
| 5 | rise, increase, go up | a rise, an increase |
| 6 | fall, drop, dip, decrease, decline | a fall, a drop, a dip, a decrease, a decline |

**B** To describe trends in more detail, you also need to say how much something goes up or down. You can do this by using adverbs to describe verbs, or adjectives to describe nouns. Look at the table on page 52 and complete the following descriptions of rainfall patterns in Cairo, New Delhi and Singapore, by selecting the correct option in each pair.

In **Singapore**, the amount of rainfall *drops/rises dramatically/slightly* from January to February. After a *slight/significant rise/fall* in March, the level of rainfall *increases/decreases steadily/sharply* until July. Over the next three months, the rainfall *reaches a peak/fluctuates sharply/slowly*. Finally, at the end of the year, we can see a *slight/dramatic rise/decline* in rainfall in November and a *leveling off/peak* in December.

In **Cairo**, the rainfall *fluctuates/remains constant* at 5mm per month from January to March. It then *declines/goes up gradually/sharply* to zero in July and August before *decreasing/rising significantly/gradually* again in the second half of the year.

In **New Delhi**, there is a *steady/slight drop/rise* in rainfall from January to March followed by a *dramatic/gradual increase/decrease* to around 170–180 mm in July and August. The final part of the year shows rainfall *falling/rising dramatically/slowly* to a *peak/low point* of 3mm in November.

**express tip**

Don't describe every small change in a graph. Decide what the general trends are. For example, over a one-year period, never describe 12 monthly changes in a graph!

**C** Are the following questions about the three paragraph descriptions in 2B true or false? Write **T** for **True** or **F** for **False**.

1 The present continuous tense is used throughout. ........

2 A regular adverb is formed with the adjective + *ly*. .......

3 Generally, adjectives come after the noun and adverbs come before the verb. .......

**D** Using the line graph on page 52 and the model provided in 2B, describe the changes in temperature in the three cities. Use the language above, as well as phrases like *there is/are ...*, *we can see ...* and *... shows ...* . Read your descriptions to a partner, but don't say the name of the city. Can your partner guess which city each description refers to?

**WRITING**

## 3 Describing trends

**A** Academic Writing Task 1 questions often ask you to compare more than one graph. The following two graphs show the climate in two cities. Use the words in the box and the information in the graphs to complete the following passage. There are more words/phrases than spaces, so you will not use them all.

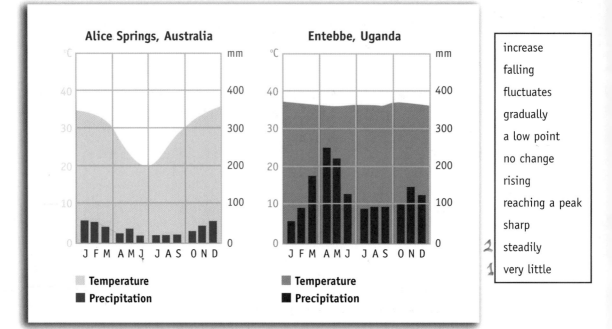

increase

falling

fluctuates

gradually

a low point

no change

rising

reaching a peak

sharp

2 steadily

1 very little

Looking first at rainfall, you can see that there is **1** ...... *very little* rain in Alice Springs, which is typical for a desert climate. There is about 50mm of rain in January and this falls **2** ...... *steadily* to approximately 20mm in August before **3** ...... again to 50mm in December. Entebbe, on the other hand, has a very different pattern. The amount of rain **4** ...... considerably over the year. In the first three months of the year, there is a very **5** ...... increase in rainfall, **6** ...... of about 250mm in April. This is followed by an equally dramatic drop to **7** ...... of about 80mm in July. For the next three months, there is **8** ...... in the amount of rain until October when it starts to **9** ...... again.

**B** Read the paragraph again.
1 What expression is used to contrast the two cities?   ..........................
2 What two words are used to describe numbers which are not exact?   ..........................

**C** When describing trends, you will need to use prepositions correctly. Complete sentences 1–5 about global warming with prepositions in the box.

| between | by | from (x2) | in (x3) | of | over | to (x2) |
|---|---|---|---|---|---|---|

# Global warming

**1** Global warming will increase average temperatures ........ 12°C ........ 13.5°C ........ the next 40 years.

**2** ........ 1980 ........ 2000 there was a 150% increase ........ greenhouse gases.

**3** ........ 1904 and 2004 there has been a rise ........ 0.5°C in global temperature.

**4** Water levels are increasing ........ 2 cm every year.

**5** Temperatures fall ........ winter and rise ........ summer.

**D** Look at the graph in 3A. Using the paragraph in 3A as a model, write a second paragraph to explain the changes in temperature in Alice Springs and Entebbe.

## 4 Academic Writing Task 1: Report

**for this task**

▸ Look carefully at the graphs/tables and try to understand what the graph is showing.

▸ Decide what tense(s) you will need to use.

▸ Look for trends and identify similarities between different countries. Determine if any countries stand out as different from the others.

▸ Don't describe every single change shown in the

graphs/tables – describe the overall trends. Remember to support your general observations with specific examples.

▸ Use a variety of language to describe trends – verbs with adverbs and nouns with adjectives.

▸ Remember you should spend 20 minutes on this task. Allow a few minutes at the end to check your work.

You should spend about 20 minutes on this task.

*The graph below shows the figures for CFC emissions in four countries between 1989 and 2001.*

*Summarise the information by selecting and reporting the main features, and make comparisons where relevant.*

Write at least 150 words.

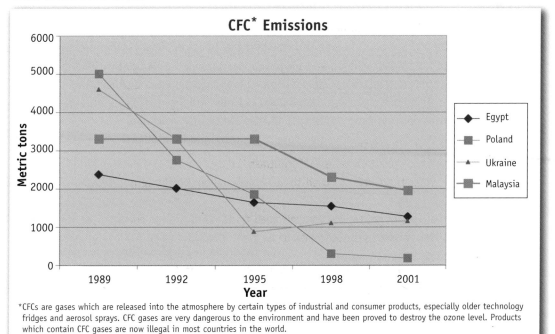

*CFCs are gases which are released into the atmosphere by certain types of industrial and consumer products, especially older technology fridges and aerosol sprays. CFC gases are very dangerous to the environment and have been proved to destroy the ozone level. Products which contain CFC gases are now illegal in most countries in the world.

# 7 Food and Diet

▶ **Exam tasks** ▶ Yes/No/Not Given; summary completion
▶ **Skill** ▶ Identifying opinions

*[handwritten notes:]*
*What are people talk about.*
*hunger / malnutrition. - too wrong thing*
*starvation - too little*
*overeating - too much*
*obese - too fat*
*Junk food (rubbish).*
*GM — made by scientists in a lab.*
*organic - natural, no chemicals*

## 1 Introduction

**A** Discuss these questions with a partner.

*[handwritten: Instructions]*

- Do you have a healthy diet? What do you eat that is healthy/unhealthy?   *[handwritten: needs vocab]*
- Have you ever bought organic food? Are there certain types of food that you avoid, e.g. GM (genetically modified) food? Why?

**B** Do you agree or disagree with the statements below? Share your views with a partner. Remember to justify your opinion. *[handwritten: = Why]*

1 Generally speaking, people know which foods are good for them.
2 The modern problem with food is not one of hunger; it is one of unhealthy eating.
3 People eat more healthily than they did twenty years ago.
4 Certain groups of people have a healthier diet than others.  *[handwritten: rich / wealth   poor]*
5 The government should tax unhealthy food.

## IN THE EXAM

**Reading module: Yes/No/Not Given; completion tasks**

In the Reading module, you may be tested on your understanding of the opinions and arguments made by the author of a passage. In this case, common task types are true/false/not given and yes/no/not given questions. true/false/not given questions were practised in Unit 1.

In the Reading module, completion tasks are very common. These can be table completion, sentence completion or summary completion tasks. In summary completion tasks, you are asked to fill in gaps in a summary with words taken directly from the reading passage or with words selected from a list of words provided.

## 2 Identifying opinions

**A** Read the following statement about organic farming.

*Organic farming is better for wildlife, causes lower pollution from sprays, produces less carbon dioxide, has high animal welfare standards and increases rural employment.*

Read sentences i–iii. For each sentence, say if it

**a** expresses the same opinion as the statement above (Yes).

**b** expresses an opposite opinion from the statement above (No).

**c** says something completely new, not mentioned in the original statement (Not Given).

.................. **i** Organic farming is harmful to the environment. *false – low pollution/CO2*

.................. **ii** The countryside benefits from organic farming. *high standards / rural emp.*

.................. **iii** Organic farming is usually more expensive. *NG*

**B** Read the following two statements. For each statement, write Yes, No or Not Given.

**1** *The benefits of GM crops tend to be overlooked; for example, they have a potential for feeding the developing world with a crop rich in essential vitamins and other nutrients.*

............. **i** GM crops have no benefits for the developing world.

............. **ii** GM crops can help improve the diet of poorer sections of the world's population.

............. **iii** GM crops are more resistant to disease.

**2** *When it comes to persuading their children to eat healthily, parents have a hard fight on their hands. How can a bowl of fresh fruit compete with the images of fizzy drinks, sweets and crisps that children see every time they turn on the TV?*

............. **i** Advertising aimed at children increases sales of fizzy drinks, sweets and crisps.

............. **ii** Parents find it easy to convince their children to eat healthy food.

............. **iii** TV advertising affects what children want to eat.

# The world's expanding waistline

WHEN the world was a simpler place, the rich were fat, the poor were thin, and people worried about how to feed the hungry. Now, in much of the world, the rich are thin, the poor are fat, and people are worrying about obesity.

Thanks to rising agricultural productivity, famine is rarer all over the globe. According to the UN, the number of people short of food fell from 920m in 1980 to 799m in 2000, even though the world's population increased by 1.6 billion over the period. But the consequence of this prosperity brings a new problem and with it a host of interesting policy dilemmas.

Obesity is the world's biggest public-health issue today – the main cause of heart disease, which kills more people these days than AIDS, malaria, war; the principal risk factor in diabetes; heavily implicated in cancer and other diseases. Since the World Health Organisation labelled obesity an 'epidemic' in 2000, there have been many reports on its fearful consequences.

Will public-health warnings, combined with media pressure, persuade people to get thinner, just as they finally put them off tobacco? There is now agreement among doctors that governments should do something to help.

## Diet by command?

There's nothing new about the idea that governments should intervene in the food business. One of the earliest examples was in 1202, when King John of England first banned the adulteration of bread. Governments and people seem to agree that ensuring the safety and stability of the food supply is part of the state's job. But obesity is a more complicated issue than food safety. It is not about ensuring that people don't get poisoned; it is about changing their behaviour. Should governments be trying to do anything about it at all?

There is a bad reason for doing something, and a couple of good ones. The bad reason is that governments should help citizens look after themselves. People, the argument goes, are misled by their bodies, which are constantly trying to store a few more calories in case of hunger in the near future. Governments should help guide them towards better eating habits. But that argument is weaker in the case of food than it is for tobacco – nicotine is addictive, chocolate is not – people have a choice of being sensible or silly. People should choose, not governments.

## Get them young

A better argument for intervention is that dietary habits are established early in childhood. Once people get fat, it is hard for them to get thin; once they are used to breakfasting on chips and Coke, it's hard to change. The state, which has some responsibility for shaping young people, should try to ensure that its small citizens aren't overdosing on sugar at primary school. Britain's government is talking about tough restrictions on advertising junk food to children. It seems unlikely that it will have much effect. Sweden already bans advertising to children, and its young people are as fat as those in comparable countries. Other moves, such as banning junk food from schools, might work better.

## The cost of obesity

A second plausible argument for intervention is that thin people subsidise fat people through health care. If everybody is forced to pay for the seriously fat, then everybody has an interest in seeing them slim down. This should not be a problem in insurance-financed health care systems, such as America's. Insurance companies should be able to charge fat people more because they cost more. That leaves the question of what should happen in a state–financed health system. Why not tax fattening food – sweets, snacks and takeaways? That might discourage consumption of unhealthy food and also get back some of the costs of obesity.

It might; but it would also be too great an intrusion on liberty for the gain in equity and efficiency it might (or might not) represent. Society has a legitimate interest in fat because fat and thin people both pay for it. But it also has a legitimate interest in not having the government interfere in people's private business. If people want to eat their way to grossness and an early grave, let them.

## 3 Yes/No/Not Given

Read the article on page 58 and answer *Questions 1–8*.

### for this task

▸ Read the questions carefully and underline the keywords in each of the statements.

▸ Scan the text for the keywords you have identified to find the relevant section in the text.

▸ Once you have located the relevant section of text, read it more carefully to decide if the writer agrees, disagrees or doesn't state an opinion about the question.

**Questions 1–8**

Do the following statements agree with the views of the writer in the passage on page 58?

*You should write*

| | |
|---|---|
| **YES** | *if the statement agrees with the views of the writer* |
| **NO** | *if the statement contradicts the views of the writer* |
| **NOT GIVEN** | *if it impossible to say what the writer thinks about this* |

**express tip**

If you can't locate an answer in the passage, it is possible that the text has no information about this question, and therefore the answer to this question is 'Not Given'.

...... **1** Increasing world population has led to famine.

...... **2** Obesity is one of the biggest killers in the world.

...... **3** Doctors should advise people on how to lose weight.

...... **4** Governments should try to prevent children from picking up bad eating habits.

...... **5** Overweight people cost health systems more, and therefore should pay health insurance.

...... **6** Overweight people should not smoke.

...... **7** Banning advertisements of junk food aimed at children would change their eating habits.

...... **8** Everyone has a right to eat what they like and as much as they like.

## 4 Summary completion

**A** How many of the writer's ideas can you remember? Without looking at the text, discuss with a partner.

**B** Look at the notes a student has made about the text. Number the notes 1–4 according to the information in the passage.

☐ Obese people cost a lot in health care
  – who pays?
  – through insurance
  – through tax on unhealthy food?

☐ Change eating habits early in childhood – therefore UK ban advertising of junk food – how effective? (compare with Sweden – no effect)

☐ More food produced today – less famine

☐ New problem of obesity – health issue

**for this task**

▸ There are two types of summary completion tasks. You may have to take words directly from the text, in which case you must not change the words, or you may have a list of words to choose from. The words in the list will have the same or similar meaning to words or phrases in the passage. The summary may focus on the whole of the passage or one section of the passage. The questions follow the same order as the information in the passage.

▸ Quickly read the summary to understand the general meaning.

▸ Make sure you use the correct number of words and spell the words correctly.

▸ For each gap, locate the relevant parts of the passage and read those sections again carefully. As you read, think about the meaning and grammar of the missing word(s). Are you looking for a verb, noun, adjective or adverb?

 **Questions 9–15**

*Complete the summary below.*

*Choose* **NO MORE THAN THREE WORDS** *from the passage for each answer.*

Farming today is much more productive than even twenty years ago, and it is due to this increase in

**9** ................................. . that famine in this time has become much less common in the world.

However, it has led to a new problem of obesity, which has become the most significant global

**10** ................................. concern.

It is generally agreed that the government should be responsible for protecting the

**11** ................................. of society's food. However, obesity is a more complicated issue and it raises

the question of whether governments should try to alter people's **12** ................................. . Many

disagree that the duty of the government is to take care of society by encouraging

**13** ................................. . Surely, people have a choice whether to eat healthily or not.

Those who favour government involvement in our food consumption think it is more effective to try to

change people while they are still at **14** ................................. . There should therefore be restrictions

on junk food being advertised to children. The problem, though, is that this has already been tried in

Sweden, and there is no difference between there and **15** ................................. .

 **Questions 16–19**

*Complete the summary below using words from the box.*

At the moment, the extra cost of health care attributable to obese people is paid by

**16** ................................. . In countries where health care is funded by insurance, this is not such

a problem because overweight people can be charged higher premiums. However, in countries which have

**17** ................................. funded medical services this is not possible. One possible solution would be

the introduction of a **18** ................................. on unhealthy food. Although this might work to reduce

obesity, it is likely to be very unpopular – most people will see it as too great an interference in personal

**19** ................................. .

| doctors | government | privacy | finance |
|---------|-----------|---------|---------|
| health | society | ruling | policy |
| citizen | freedom | individuals | company |
| choice | diet | levy | business |

> ▶ **Exam focus** ▶ Speaking Part 2: Individual long turn; Speaking Part 3: Two-way discussion
>
> ▶ **Skills** ▶ Describing an experience; generating ideas

# 1 Introduction

Discuss these questions with a partner.

*Tasty / Greasy / Spicy (Hot)*
*Watery /*

1 What's your favourite food? Is there any food you really hate?

2 When was the last time you ate out? Where did you go? Can you remember what you ordered?

*← cuisines*

# 2 Describing an experience

A Read the topic card below. Then close your eyes for 15 seconds and 'see and feel yourself' in this situation. Don't speak during this time.

> **Describe a recent restaurant experience.**
> **You should say:**
>   **where you ate**
>   **who you went with**
>   **what you ate**
> **and explain how you felt about the experience.**

**express tip**

To save time in the exam, use note form to label your mind map. Don't write full sentences.

B After visualising the scene, take notes in as much detail as possible in preparation for a two-minute talk. For examples of students' notes, see page 30.

C The topic card you are given in Part 2 provides a way to organise your thoughts, but you will often want to (or need to) add extra information, which is not on the card.

1 What extra information could you usefully include in your talk about the topic on the card in 2A? Discuss with a partner.

## IN THE EXAM

### Speaking module: Part 2

In Part 2 of the Speaking exam, you are given a card and you are asked to talk about your experiences and feelings – this will often mean describing a real situation in the past from a personal viewpoint. You are given one minute to prepare your talk.

For more information on Part 2 of the Speaking exam, see unit 3.

**2**  **7.1**  Listen to an IELTS candidate giving a talk on the topic card in 2A, and tick (✔) the information that the student provides.

|   |   |   |   |
|---|---|---|---|
| **a** when he went | ☐ | **e** how often he goes there | ☐ |
| **b** what the weather was like | ☐ | **f** what his friend ate | ☐ |
| **c** how he was dressed | ☐ | **g** how much he paid for the meal | ☐ |
| **d** what he did before going to the restaurant | ☐ | **h** what his friend thought of the meal | ☐ |

**3**  The points on the topic card are often presented in a logical order, e.g. first, provide a context, then describe the events and finally, give your feelings and opinions. Write the extra information (a–h) the student provided under the correct heading in the table below.

> **express tip**
>
> Use words like *any-way*, *so* and *well* to change the direction of your talk and indicate you are moving to a new topic.

| Context | Events | Feelings |
|---|---|---|
| where he went/who he went with | what he ate | what he thought of the meal |
| a.............................. | .............................. | .............................. |

**D**  Use the topic card and your notes to talk to your partner for at least one minute. Remember to structure your talk by following the order of the points on the card.

## 3  Individual long turn

### *for this task*

Read the card and try to visualise a real situation that you have personally experienced. Make sure you cover all the points on the card. Present extra information in a logical order. In describing an experience, we generally first describe the context, then describe events and finally explain reasons. Try to think about any extra information you want to include before you start your talk and include it in your notes or mind map. Use 'signposts' to 'change direction' in your talk, and remember that you are describing a personal experience, so you will need to talk about your feelings.

Work in pairs. Practise the interview for two minutes.

**Student A:** You are the candidate. For one minute, look at the topic card below and prepare notes. Then, use your notes to speak for one or two minutes. Follow the advice in *for this task*.

**Student B:** You are the examiner. Give student B one minute to look at the card below and make notes. Then listen to student B's answers carefully. Does he or she follow the advice in *for this task*?
After one or two minutes, interrupt and ask student B a few questions related to the topic.

When you have finished, change roles.

> **express tip**
>
> You need to speak for at least one minute. The examiner will let you know when it is time to stop.

> **Describe a memorable meal.**
> **You should say:**
>     what you ate
>     what the occasion was
>     what happened during the meal
> **and explain why the meal was memorable.**

## 4 Generating ideas

A Do you agree or disagree with the opinion below? Share your views with a partner. Remember to justify your opinion.

*Fast food should have health warnings like cigarettes.*

B Work in pairs. With a partner, discuss the following six questions which are related to the opinion above.

| **express tip** |
|---|
| When thinking of your opinion, think of five 'w's and one 'h': *what, where, when, who, why* and *how*. |

**Who** decides what is written on the health warnings?

**Why** are they necessary?

**What** should be written on the health warnings?

**'Do you think fast food should have health warnings like cigarettes?'**

**Where** should the health warnings be placed?

**How** can the health warnings work?

**When** should they be introduced – immediately or in stages?

C Read the opinion below and write six questions (who, what, where, when, why, how) about it. Then discuss your questions with a partner.

*Fast food companies should not be allowed to target children in their advertising.*

## 5 Two-way discussion

Work in pairs. Practise the two-way discussion.

**7.2** **Student A:** Listen to questions 1–3 on the recording. After each question, there will be a pause to give you time to answer. Direct your answers to student B. Follow the advice in *for this task*.

**7.3** **Student B:** Listen to your partner's response to the question. Does he or she give full, detailed responses? Now listen to questions 4–6 on the recording. After each question, there will be a pause to give you time to answer. Direct your answers to student A. Follow the advice in *for this task*.

**IN THE EXAM**

**Speaking module: Part 3**

In Part 2 of the Speaking exam, you are asked to talk about your experiences, while in Part 3 you are asked to express your opinion on the topic. For more information about Speaking Part 3, see Unit 5.

# Sickness and Health

> ▶ **Exam tasks** ▶ Labelling a diagram; multiple-choice questions
> ▶ **Exam focus** ▶ Listening Section 4: Academic monologue
> ▶ **Skills** ▶ Understanding description; identifying differences between pictures

## 1 Introduction

**A** Work in pairs. Look at the following lists of words. Which word is the 'odd one out' in each group?

1 block, faculty, treatment, unit, ward
2 doctor, nurse, patient, surgery
3 illness, disease, disorder, cure
4 administration, obstetrics, gynaecology, pathology
5 architecture, intensive care, radiography, paediatrics

**B** What else might you find in a hospital? Make a list with a partner.

## 2 Understanding description

**A 1** Look at the diagram of a hospital on page 65 and describe the layout to your partner. Use the expressions in the box below.

| there is/are | opposite | at the end | the first/second/third/fourth (building) on the left/right |
| on the left/right | at the bottom/top | in the left/right (hand) corner | |
| in front of | in the middle | | |

**2** Look at the labels. Are they numbered left to right, bottom to top or clockwise?
**3** How are *Questions 1–5* different from *Questions 6–10*?
**4** Look at the box of answers for *Questions 1–5*. Practise saying the words to yourself so that you can recognise them if you hear them on the recording.

---

### IN THE EXAM

**Listening module: Section 4**

Section 4 of the Listening module is an academic monologue, for example, a university lecture.

Common task types in Section 4 are note completion,

labelling a diagram and multiple-choice with pictures. In labelling tasks, you are asked to label parts of a diagram or plan. In multiple-choice with pictures, you are asked to choose the picture which best represents the correct answer to a question.

**B** (8.1) Now listen to the first part of a lecture on hospital design and answer *Questions 1–5*. Remember you don't need to write the full name, just the code provided.

**Questions 1–5**

*Label the plan below.*

*Write the correct code next to Questions 1–5.*

| | | | |
|---|---|---|---|
| **AB** | Administration Block | **L** | Laboratories |
| **FM** | Faculty of Medicine | **OGU** | Obstetrics and Gynaecology Unit |
| **ICU** | Intensive Care Unit | **PU** | Pathology Unit |
| **IMU** | Internal Medicine Unit | **UDD** | Unit for Digestive Disorders |

**C** Look at *Questions 6–10* below. Work in pairs.

**1** What question does each label ask you? For example, *Question 6*, 'Who/What is treated … ?'

**2** Underline the keywords in the question and think of any synonyms or paraphrases you might hear on the recording.

**3** What kind of answer are you listening for?

**D** (8.2) Now listen to the second part of the lecture and answer *Questions 6–10*. Write your answer in the space provided on each label. Write no more than three words for each label.

**Questions 6–10**

*Label the diagram below. Write **NO MORE THAN THREE WORDS** for each answer.*

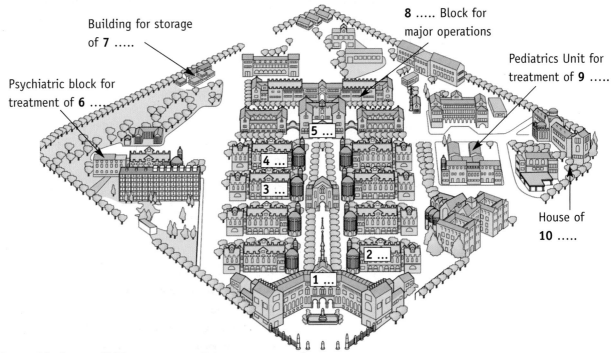

Building for storage of **7** .....

**8** ..... Block for major operations

Psychiatric block for treatment of **6** .....

Pediatrics Unit for treatment of **9** .....

House of **10** .....

5 ...

4 ...

3 ...

2 ...

1 ...

## 3 Identifying differences between pictures

**A** Look at pictures A–D on page 66 and discuss these questions with a partner.

**1** What do they have in common?

**2** In what way are they different? Can you describe what the difference is?

**3** What are the keywords for each picture?

 B **8.3** Listen and answer *Question 1.*

**Question 1**

Listen to a doctor giving a report on the condition of a patient involved in a road accident, and tick the picture that best represents the patient's condition.

A     B     C     D

## 4   Labelling a diagram

### for this task

There are two kinds of labelling tasks. In matching questions, you need to match features of the diagram to items from a list. In label completion questions, you are asked to fill a gap in a label, usually with three words or less.

**Before you listen**

▶ Read the instructions to see how many words you should use to complete each gap.

▶ Look at the diagram. Describe it in your own words.

▶ Identify the keywords on the label. Think of synonyms you might hear on the recording. Try to predict the answer.

**As you listen**

▶ Keep track of the part of the diagram being described by pointing to each part as you hear it discussed on the recording.

▶ When you hear the keyword or any of its synonyms, listen out for the answer. Write your answer in the space provided.

You will hear a medical school lecturer introducing first year students to the major organs of the body and describing their function. Answer *Questions 1–6* by labelling the diagram.

 **8.4** *Questions 1–6*
*Label the diagram below.*
Write **NO MORE THAN THREE WORDS**
*for each answer.*

**Model of human torso**

**Lungs:** take 2 ..Oxygen.. from air and put it into the blood

**Trachea** (1 carries air... ): carries air from mouth and nose to lungs

**Heart:** pumps blood round the body

**Liver:** separates toxic from useful substances

**Intestines:** absorb 3 ..nutrions.. and collect waste material

**Kidneys:** 4 ✗........ and pass it into urine

**Bladder:** a 5 ..kind of bag.. for urine

## 5 Multiple-choice (pictures); multiple-choice with multiple answers

### for this task

**Multiple-choice with multiple answers**

Some multiple-choice questions require you to choose more than one answer from a range of options. You may be asked to choose 2 answers from 5 options or 4 answers from 7 options. Approach these in the same way as multiple-choice with single answer questions. Be careful to note how many answers you must give.

▶ Study the pictures. What are the key differences between them? Identify the parts of the picture and any synonyms or paraphrases to describe those parts.

▶ Listen for any of the keywords or synonyms you identified earlier. Don't select an option just because you hear a keyword mentioned on the recording. The pictures are likely to be quite similar. You need to listen for those features that make the pictures different.

 **8.5** *Questions 1–2*

*Choose the correct picture, **A**, **B**, **C** or **D**.*

**1** How should a fainting victim be positioned?

**2** How should the head be positioned to make sure the breathing passage is not blocked?

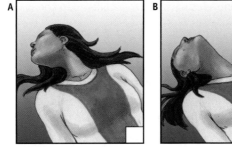 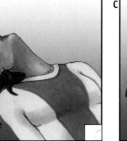  

 **8.6** *Questions 3–4*

*Choose **TWO** letters, **A–E**.*

*Which **TWO** items should medical students **NOT** take with them to the hospital?*

**A** a car

**B** a thermometer

**C** a stethoscope

**D** a white coat

**E** a mobile phone

## WRITING

▶ **Exam task** ▶ 'Agree or disagree' essay

▶ **Exam focus** ▶ Academic Writing Task 2 ▶ For additional General Training Task 2 practice, go to page 80.

▶ **Skills** ▶ Supporting your statements and opinions; brainstorming arguments for and against; structuring an 'agree or disagree' essay

# 1 Introduction

**A** Work in pairs. Match the vocabulary in the box with the appropriate category.

**Illness and cures:** get/have flu, ......................................................................................................

..........................................................................................................................................................

**Methods of prevention:** reduce stress, ........................................................................................

..........................................................................................................................................................

| | | |
|---|---|---|
| be a positive thinker | get/have HIV/Aids | stop smoking |
| die of cancer | have an operation | take antibiotics |
| eat a balanced diet | immunise against disease | take medicine |
| get a vaccination | reduce stress | take up sport |
| get/have flu | sleep well | undergo surgery |

**B** Can you think of any other words or expressions for each category? Discuss with a partner.

# 2 Supporting your statements and opinions

**A** Statements and opinions need to be supported by facts, examples or arguments. Complete sentences 1–5 with the supporting information a–e.

**1** Eating a balanced diet is much better than taking medicine

**2** I disagree with the idea of flu vaccinations

---

## IN THE EXAM

### Academic Writing module: Task 2

'Agree or disagree' questions are the most common questions in both IELTS Academic and General Training modules. You can either answer them like a 'for and against essay', looking at both sides of the argument (see Unit 4), or you can put forward your own personal opinion and take

one side of the argument, i.e. 'agree or disagree'.

You should write at least 250 words. There is no choice of questions. It provides two thirds of the mark for the writing test, so you should spend two thirds of the time (40 minutes) on this part of the exam.

**3** I believe that positive thinking can help you overcome illness, including cancer

**4** Many people think that reducing stress is the key to improving your health

**5** It's generally believed that taking up sport is a good idea

    **a** ...... because in my experience they don't often work.

    **b** ...... because you are preventing illness, not simply curing it.

    **c** ...... as it reduces the chances of a heart attack.

    **d** ...... since it helps you lose weight and keeps you fit.

    **e** ...... as many studies of patients have proved this to be true.

**B** Provide support for statements 1–5.

    **1** It's more important to spend money on Aids research than cancer research ...

    **2** I think that smokers often have colds ...

    **3** It's generally understood that senior businesspeople suffer a lot from stress ...

    **4** Waiting lists to undergo surgery are too long ...

    **5** I believe that people who do not vaccinate their children are irresponsible ...

## 3 Brainstorming arguments for and against

**A** Read this statement and decide if you agree or disagree.

*In some countries in the world, health service is free.*

*Some people feel that smokers should not get free treatment for smoking related illnesses because they are knowingly harming themselves.*

**B** Using your own ideas, knowledge and experience, make a list of arguments to support your opinion.

> I agree/disagree with the statement.
>
> Arguments to support my position:

- ................................................................................................
- ................................................................................................
- ................................................................................................
- ................................................................................................
- ................................................................................................

**C** Compare and discuss your answers with a partner.

## 4 Structuring an 'agree or disagree' essay

**A** Skim essays 1 and 2 on the following page and decide if they agree or disagree with the statement in the exam question in 3A.

**B** Read essays 1 and 2 again. Can you identify any arguments or points that are similar to yours in 3B? Tell your partner. Has your opinion changed in any way after reading these two essays?

### Essay 1

**A** As a non-smoker myself, I totally agree with this statement that smokers should pay for any treatment for smoking-related illnesses. Smokers know the risk of smoking, so why should society have to pick up the bill?

**B** Looking at the smokers' argument, they say that they should receive free health treatment like everyone else because they also pay taxes like everyone else. However, I don't think this argument is valid because they are using many more health services than non-smokers, but they pay the same amount in taxes. Smokers also say that they pay very high cigarette taxes, which covers the cost of higher health costs for smokers. I disagree with this too, because in many countries people buy cigarettes on the black market at a very low price, and so the government receives no money in taxes.

**C** Smokers are killing themselves and killing other people too. Smokers pay more for life insurance and health insurance to private companies, so it is fair that they also pay more for treatment in the public health service. In fact, they should be contributing to the health care of non-smokers too as passive smoking causes major health problems.

**D** To summarise, I would say that it is right that smokers pay extra for all the extra costs that they place on society. If smokers paid more money to cover their extra health costs, it would help smokers and the government. Unfortunately, it would not help non-smokers as we have to breathe in their smoke every day in bars and restaurants and at work. I think smokers should pay more taxes, and the government should ban smoking in all public places too!

### Essay 2

**A** I completely disagree with the idea that smokers should not receive free treatment for smoking-related illnesses if other people in the country are receiving free medical treatment without any limits or conditions. Is it right for smokers to pay, while drug addicts and alcoholics receive expensive medical treatment free?

**B** Anti-smokers think that smokers have chosen a 'dangerous lifestyle' and should therefore not expect free health treatment paid for from general taxes. The problem with this argument is that we are making a judgement about someone's lifestyle before we decide to give them free treatment or not. Do we refuse to give medical treatment to someone who has a car accident driving dangerously on the motorway without a seatbelt? Of course not. Most reasonable people would argue that it is impossible to decide who has a 'dangerous lifestyle' and who does not.

**C** Smokers already pay a huge amount to the government every time they buy a packet of cigarettes through cigarette taxes. In Greece for example, we pay over 50% tax on cigarettes which means that I pay two euros to the government for every packet of cigarettes I buy. The government uses some of that money to finance the health service, so why shouldn't I get free health treatment? I pay more money in taxes than a non-smoker, so I should get more from the health system. That is logical.

**D** In conclusion, I would say that it is very important that smokers are treated in the same way as other people. It is very dangerous to say that someone's right to free health treatment should be on the basis of their lifestyle. Who is going to play God and decide whether a particular lifestyle is 'good' or 'bad'? And who is going to decide whether you should live or die?

C Both essays are organised in the same way. Skim the essays again. Match the paragraphs (A–D) with the paragraph descriptions (1–4).

....... 1 Briefly summarise your arguments and re-emphasise your opinion.

....... 2 List your arguments to support your opinion.

....... 3 Clearly state your agreement/disagreement and rewrite the original question in your own words.

....... 4 Briefly state the opposing arguments and attack this position.

D Look at the useful language structures highlighted in the essays. Find an example of the writing features below. There may be more than one example for each of the writing features.

---

**Essay writing features**

1 signpost words to indicate final paragraph

2 open question that supports your position

3 question (with answer) that supports your opinion

4 personal experience to support your opinion

5 opposing an argument

6 phrase to express agreement/disagreement with essay question

---

## 5 Academic and General Training: Essay

### for this task

- Read the question and decide if you personally agree or disagree with the statement.

- Take three to four minutes to note down your points to support your position (agree or disagree). You will also need to note down one or two opposing arguments in order to attack them.

- Use the simple four-paragraph organisational structure. See section 4C.

- Use some of the writing features in 4D, like using questions and personal experience to support your arguments, using punctuation and short sentences to add impact, etc.

- Allow a few minutes at the end to read through and check your essay.

You should spend about 40 minutes on this task.

Write about the following topic:

*Governments around the world spend too much money on treating illnesses and diseases and not enough on health education and prevention.*

*Do you agree or disagree with this statement?*

Give reasons for your answer and include any relevant examples from your own knowledge or experience.

Write at least 250 words.

▶ **Exam task** ▶ Writing a letter of request
▶ **Exam focus** ▶ General Training Writing Task 1
▶ **Skills** ▶ Recognising types of letters; planning a letter; using appropriate language and organisation

## 1 Introduction

Discuss these questions with a partner.

• When did you last write a letter? Who was it to, and why did you write it? What did you write about?

• Why do you think people write letters?

## 2 Recognising types of letters

**A** Read the opening sentences of the letters below.

> *express tip*
>
> It's common to use short forms (*I'll, she'd, they're,* etc.) in informal and semi-formal letters.

**1** Dear Sir/Madam,

I am writing to enquire about your courses in Business Studies starting next year.

**2** Hi Andrea,

How are you doing? Can you let me have a copy of your report by the end of the week? We've got a presentation on Monday and it would be really useful.

**3** Dear Mr White,

I have been a customer of yours for several years. However, I am writing to complain about the quality of service I received at your bank last week.

**4** Dear Ms Davis,

I am writing to let you know that unfortunately I cannot start my studies as planned at the beginning of the academic year.

**5** Dear Mr and Mrs Johnson,

I am a member of the Student Exchange Programme, and I'm writing to tell you a little bit about myself as I'll be coming to stay with your family next month.

## IN THE EXAM

### General Training: Writing Task 1

In Writing Task 1 of the General Training module, you are required to write a letter, usually based on a situation related to living and studying abroad. You may be asked to complain, explain or enquire about something, to request information or to introduce yourself. You will need to write a minimum of 150 words, include relevant details and use appropriate language and style so that the purpose of your letter is clear to the reader. There is no choice of questions. Task 1 provides one third of the mark for the writing exam, so you should spend no more than one third of the time on this part of the exam (20 minutes).

**B** What is the main purpose of each letter? Match the opening sentences (1–5) to the purpose of each letter.

........................ requesting information ........................ introducing yourself

........................ making a complaint ........................ explaining a situation

........................ requesting a favour

**C** What is the relationship between the writer and the reader of each letter? Are they friends, student and teacher? Is each letter formal, semi-formal or informal? Discuss your ideas with a partner.

**D** Which of the following endings is the most appropriate for each letter? Match the endings (a–e) with the opening sentences of the letters 1–5.

1 ............    2 ..............    3 ..............    4 ..............    5 ..............

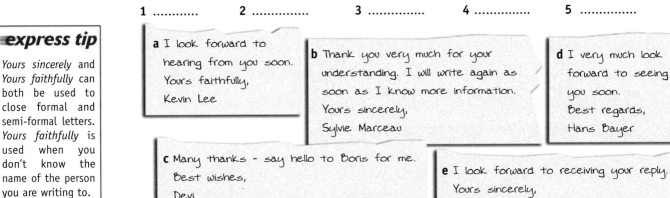

**a** I look forward to hearing from you soon.
Yours faithfully,
Kevin Lee

**b** Thank you very much for your understanding. I will write again as soon as I know more information.
Yours sincerely,
Sylvie Marceau

**d** I very much look forward to seeing you soon.
Best regards,
Hans Bayer

**c** Many thanks – say hello to Boris for me.
Best wishes,
Devi

**e** I look forward to receiving your reply.
Yours sincerely,
Anjelica Martin

**express tip**

*Yours sincerely* and *Yours faithfully* can both be used to close formal and semi-formal letters. *Yours faithfully* is used when you don't know the name of the person you are writing to.

## 3 Planning a letter

**A** Study the exam question below. What is the main purpose of this letter? What is the relationship between the person writing the letter and the reader? What is the level of formality required? Discuss with a partner.

> *As an international student in Australia, you have an account with a local bank. The monthly bank transfer you receive from your parents has been delayed this month due to an error at your parents' bank.*
>
> *Write a letter to your bank. In your letter*
> • *introduce yourself and ask for a loan (a)*
> • *say why you need the money (b)*
> • *tell them how you intend to pay back the money. (c)*

**B** Imagine you are the student speaking to your bank manager. What would you say to him or her? Discuss your ideas with a partner.

**express tip**

You will need to use your imagination to come up with details to include in your letter, but the details must be relevant to the situation.

**C** Study the following list of points. Decide which five points are the most relevant to include when answering the exam question above.

1 Student at Sydney University – Business

2 Enjoy my studies – always get good grades

3 Interested in travelling around Australia

4 Need to pay landlord rent

5 Bank transfer delayed – banking error

6 Need temporary loan – 1 month

7 When bank transfer arrives – repay loan

**D** Match the points you identified in 3C with the bulleted points (a–c) of the exam question.

**E** Can you think of any other information to include in your letter? Write notes for the three bulleted points (a–c) in the exam question.

(a) ...................................................................................................................................

(b) ...................................................................................................................................

(c) ...................................................................................................................................

**F** Use your notes and the handwritten notes in 3C to write full sentences.

I am a student at Sydney University studying Business
.......................................................................................................................................

.......................................................................................................................................

.......................................................................................................................................

.......................................................................................................................................

.......................................................................................................................................

.......................................................................................................................................

## 4 Using appropriate language and organisation

**A** Most formal and semi-formal letters are organised in the following way:

**1** In the opening paragraph, you introduce yourself and state the reason for writing the letter.

**2** In the main paragraph(s), you describe or explain the situation or problem.

**3** In the closing paragraph, you ask the reader to take action.

Read the sample letter below, and discuss these questions with a partner.

• Does the letter follow the standard structure outlined above?

• Has the writer included all the relevant information?

Dear Sir/Madam,

I am an international student from Malaysia studying Business Administration at Sydney University. I have had my account with you for about two years since I arrived in Australia and have always kept this account in credit. I am writing to you as I would like to request a temporary loan so that I can meet my expenses this month.

My parents send me a regular bank transfer of $2000 every month. Until now, I have always received this monthly bank transfer without any difficulty. Unfortunately, however, there has been an error at the bank branch in Kuala Lumpur and so my parents have not been able to send me the money this month. This will be a problem for me because I have to pay rent to my landlord of $800 per month which is due next week. I also need money to cover general living expenses, such as transport to and from college, etc.

I estimate that I will be able to keep my living expenses down to $600 this month in order to save money. I would therefore like to request a temporary loan of $1400 for a maximum period of one month until my parents' bank transfer arrives. Your assistance would be greatly appreciated.

I look forward very much to hearing from you soon.

Best wishes

Zainab Ahmad

**B** These are guidelines that you should follow when writing a formal or semi-formal letter. Which guideline has not been followed in the sample letter on page 74?

**1** Write one paragraph for each of the bullet points in the exam question.

**2** Start each paragraph at the left margin.

**3** Leave a blank line between paragraphs.

**4** Sign the letter with your first and last names.

**5** Use the same level of formality for the opening and the ending of the letter.

**6** Use an appropriate phrase to finish main body of letter (after the closing paragraph).

**C** Formal letters use formal language. Find examples of formal language in the sample letter above which mean the same as the following:

**1** I want to ask for ..................

**2** Sadly, the bank made a mistake ..................

**3** I think I can ..................

**4** If you can help, I'd be really happy ..................

**5** I'd like to get your reply quickly ..................

## 5 General Training Writing Task 1: Letter

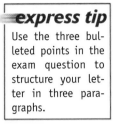 **for this task**

> Look carefully at the key words in the exam question in order to understand the reason for writing the letter.

> Decide what level of formality you should use, based on your understanding of the relationship between you and the person you are writing to.

> Use appropriate expressions at the beginning and end of your letter. When you use *Dear Sir/Madam*, end with *Yours faithfully*; for formal letters where you know the person's name (*Dear Ms Tan*, etc.), use *Yours sincerely*; for

informal or semi-formal letters (*Dear Kelly*, etc.) use *Best regards*, *Kind regards*, or *Best wishes*.

> Use the bulleted parts of the question as a guide for structuring your letter. Try to follow a simple, three-paragraph structure. Plan each paragraph of your letter in note form, and use your imagination to add any relevant details that are not listed in the question.

> Remember that for Writing Task 1, you only have about 20 minutes in total. Make sure you allow yourself a few minutes at the end to check your spelling, punctuation and grammar.

You should spend about 20 minutes on this task.

> *You are going to visit Manchester in the UK for a short training course but you have not arranged accommodation yet.*

> *Write a letter to the accommodation office of your future college. In your letter*

- *introduce yourself*
- *explain what type of accommodation you are looking for*
- *request information on that type of accommodation.*

Write at least 150 words.

You do **NOT** need to write any addresses.

Begin your letter as follows:

Dear Sir/Madam,

# Writing a Letter of Complaint

> ▶ **Exam task** ▶ Writing a letter of complaint
> ▶ **Exam focus** ▶ General Training Writing Task 1
> ▶ **Skills** ▶ Beginning a letter of complaint; imagining the situation; describing past events; giving reasons for a complaint

## 1 Introduction

Discuss these questions with a partner.

• When was the last time you complained about something? Did you express your complaint verbally or in writing? What was the situation and what did you say?

• What do you think are the most common types of written complaint?

## 2 Beginning a letter of complaint

**A** The following letters are from people who have just returned from holiday. What is each person complaining about? Match the letters (1–3) to the complaints.

........... hotel staff          ........... a hotel room          ........... a travel delay

**express tip**

Try to memorise the phrases in **bold** for introducing letters of complaint.

1 I am writing to express my disappointment regarding the standard of accommodation that your company arranged for my holiday in Malta last month.

2 I am writing to express my total dissatisfaction and frustration with the amount of time I had to wait for my flight to Rome last week.

3 I am writing to complain about the level of customer service at your hotel during my stay last weekend.

**B** Who do you think each person is complaining to? Match the letters (1–3) to the businesses.

........... package holiday company          ........... hotel          ........... airline

**C** Which writer feels the most strongly about his/her complaint? How does he/she express it? Discuss with a partner.

## IN THE EXAM

In General Training Writing Task 1, you may be required to write a letter of complaint or a letter of explanation to an organisation, company or individual. To do this, you will need to describe a sequence of events in the past and express your feelings. Your writing will be assessed according to content, organisation and use of language. The assessment criteria are the same for the Academic and General Training Writing module.

## 3 Imagining the situation

**A** Study the exam question below and discuss these questions with a partner.
- What is the purpose of this letter?
- What is the relationship between the writer and the reader?

> *You are a student at an English language school in London and are living in private accommodation with other flatmates. You have not had hot water or heating for some time. The landlord's workmen have tried to fix the problem but without success.*
>
> *Write a letter to the landlord. In your letter*
>
> - *state your reason for writing*
> - *describe the problems and explain how you feel*
> - *propose a solution and ask the landlord to take action.*

**express tip**

Asking yourself questions about each part of the exam task will help you 'see and feel' the scene, before you start writing.

**B** Work in pairs. Imagine that one of you is the tenant and the other the landlord. The tenant has decided to phone the landlord. Role-play the telephone conversation. The tenant should cover the following points:

1 Why are you contacting the landlord? .................................

2 What are the problems? .................................

3 How do the problems affect you personally? .................................

4 What do you want from the landlord? .................................

**C** Note down the language that the tenant used during the conversation.

## 4 Describing past events

**A** Read the letter below. Does it contain the information that came up during the role-play in 3B? What additional information has been included?

Dear Mr Smith,

I am one of the tenants at your property in Brick Lane, and am writing to complain about the fact that we do not have any hot water or heating in our house.

As you know, we have been living in this house **1** ...... June and have always paid our rent on time. However, we have now been without heating or hot water **2** ....... . This is making our lives very uncomfortable, especially as it is now the middle of winter. **3** ...... you said you would send a workman to our house within **4** ...... , but no one came. **5** ...... calling many times, the workman **6** ...... arrived at the house **7** ....... . Unfortunately, he said he could not fix the problem because the water heater was too old! We are **8** ...... extremely unhappy about this situation.

We are prepared to continue to rent your house but we would ask you to fix the problem **9** ....... . We also request a 50% discount on our rent for the period we have been without any hot water or heating.

We look forward to hearing from you **10** ....... .

Svetlana Asimov

**express tip**

For letters of explanation or complaint, you will need to use time expressions like *first*, *then* and *ten days ago* to describe the order in which events occurred.

**B** Now use the words and expressions in the box to complete the letter.

| soon | since | for two weeks | immediately | eventually |
|------|-------|---------------|-------------|------------|
| ten days ago | now | two days | after | five days later |

## 5 Giving reasons for a complaint

**A** Indirect speech is used to report what someone says, writes or thinks. Read the dialogue between Svetlana and her landlord, Mr Smith. Then read Svetlana's letter to Mr Smith. Notice the difference between direct and indirect speech in the dialogue and letter below. How is indirect speech formed?

Hello, Mr Smith. Unfortunately, our heating system has broken down.

Don't worry. I'll send someone round in the next two days.

**Ten days later**

Dear Mr Smith,
You said you would send someone round to fix the heating in the next two days, but no one came!

*express tip*

When imagining the situation surrounding the exam question, try to make up conversations like this, which you can include as evidence in your letter.

**B** Read the letter in 4A again and find another example of indirect speech. What do you think were the exact words the person used?

..............................................
..............................................

**C** Imagine you are one of Mr Smith's tenants. Mr Smith made a lot of promises to you when you signed the contract on the house nine months ago. Remind Mr Smith what he said.

**1** 'I am a responsible landlord.'
You told us that
.........................................................................

**2** 'I've just installed a new heating and hot water system.'
You said
.........................................................................

**3** 'You are going to be very happy here!'

.........................................................................

**4** 'My workmen have always done an excellent job fixing any problems.'

.........................................................................

## 6 General Training Writing Task 1: Letter

### for this task

▸ Remember that you should only spend about 20 minutes on this task, including time for planning and checking at the end. You need to write at least 150 words.

▸ Read the question carefully and try to imagine the situation. Ask yourself questions for each bulleted point in the exam question to help you prepare and target your letter.

▸ You are normally given three bulleted points in the exam question. You can use the different parts of the question to help you structure your letter in paragraphs. Be sure to specify your proposed solution in the last part of your letter.

▸ Include specific details with appropriate time expressions to explain the sequence of events. Try to imagine what people may have said or what brochures may have promised, etc., to use as evidence in your letter.

You should spend about 20 minutes on this task.

*You are a student at a language school in New Zealand studying Business English. Part of the course is a summer work placement programme. Unfortunately, you have just learnt from the school that this programme has now been cancelled.*

*Write a letter to the School Principal. In your letter*

- *state your reason for writing*
- *describe the problem and your concerns*
- *explain what you would like the Principal to do.*

Write at least 150 words.

You do **NOT** need to write any addresses.

Begin your letter as follows:

Dear Sir/Madam,

# Writing a General Training Essay

> ▸ **Exam task** ▸ Writing a General Training essay
> ▸ **Exam focus** ▸ General Training Writing Task 2
> ▸ **Skills** ▸ Approaching the question; organising your essay; introducing and concluding your essay

## 1 Introduction

**A** Look at the statements below. What arguments can you think of to support each viewpoint? Make a list of arguments for statements 1–5.

**1** Television has a negative influence on children.

**2** Family members are the most important people in our lives.

**3** We have a responsibility to look after the elderly people in our family or community.

**4** Single sex schools provide a better learning environment than mixed sex schools.

**B** Discuss your ideas with a partner. How similar are your opinions?

## 2 Approaching the question

**express tip**

Before you start writing your essay, use an 'a-b-c' approach: **a**nalyse the question, **b**rainstorm ideas and **c**hoose what information to include.

**A** Read the exam question below and underline the keywords.

> *It is often argued that our family is the most important thing in our lives.*
> *Why is our family so important? Which other people in our lives are important to us? Why?*
>
> Give reasons for your answer and include any relevant examples from your own knowledge or experience.

Which of the following points would you include in a 250-word answer to this question? Put a tick (✔) next to the points that you should include.

**1** Explain what are the most important things in your life. ❑

**2** Explain why you think family is important. ❑

**3** Describe the importance of your own family to you. ❑

**4** Give some examples of people who are not 'family' but who are important to you. ❑

**5** Explain why these other people are important. ❑

## IN THE EXAM

In General Training Writing Task 2, candidates are provided with a statement of a point of view, argument or problem about a specific topic. The topics chosen are of general interest, and are often related to social or cultural issues, such as family relationships, care for the elderly, smoking, etc. The question may take the form of an agree/disagree question (see Units 4 and 8), a statement for which you need to provide and explain your opinion or a problem for which you need to offer a solution. There is no choice of question and you need to write at least 250 words. Task 2 provides two thirds of the marks for the Writing module, so you should spend about two thirds of the time on this part (40 minutes).

**B** Here is another example.

> *Festivals play an important social and cultural role in many societies around the world. What is the most important festival in your country? How is the festival celebrated and why is it so important?*

Read the exam question and put a tick (✔) next to the points (1–5) that you should include.

1 Give your opinion of what you think is the world's most popular festival. ❑

2 Describe the last festival you attended in your country. ❑

3 Describe the most important festival in your country. ❑

4 Explain what happens at the festival in your country. ❑

5 Give your opinion on why this festival is an important time of the year. ❑

**C** Below is an example word web about a well-known festival in England.

**History**
- Plot to kill King James I$^{st}$ of England 400 yrs ago.
- Plan: to put gunpowder under Houses of Parliament
- Guy Fawkes and others caught - executed

**What?** Guy Fawkes' Night

**Festival: Bonfire Night**

- Children make a model of Guy Fawkes from old clothes/newspapers
- Big fire (bonfire) and fireworks display. Burn 'Guy' on fire
- Eat sausages, potatoes, special sweets - treacle

- social event - community event in winter, fun for both children and adults
- historic significance - importance of leaders and the law for social stability
- Guy Fawkes as early terrorist - has new significance?

*express tip*

Remember! You only have 250 words and 40 minutes for this task, so you will need to choose carefully the information that will be most useful to include.

Now make a similar word web about a festival from your country. Include as many details as you can, and any keywords or phrases that you would like to use in your essay.

**D** Look at the word web about Bonfire Night again. Do you think all the points are relevant to answering the exam question?

**E** Now do the same for the information in your own word web. Have you covered all parts of the question?

## 3  Organising your essay

**A** The essay on page 82 is divided into five sections A–E.  What is the purpose of each paragraph? Match paragraphs A–E to 1–5 below.

1 It explains why the festival is popular. ........C.........

2 It explains why the festival is significant. ....................

3 It describes what the festival is and when it occurs. ....................

4 It describes briefly the historical background. ....................

5 It gives an overall analysis and states the writer's opinion. ....................

**A**

One of the most popular celebrations in England is Bonfire Night, or Guy Fawkes' Night, which is held every year on November 5th. As with many other popular festivals worldwide, Bonfire Night is an important historical tradition, as well as an opportunity for people to celebrate.

**B**

On Bonfire Night, people remember an important event in English history, known as the Gunpowder Plot. Four hundred years ago, a group of men tried to blow up the Houses of Parliament during a visit by King James 1st. Fortunately for the king, the group members were caught before they could carry out their plan, and Guy Fawkes and other members of the group were executed.

**C**

Since that time, English people have celebrated the king's lucky escape every year by building large fires called 'bonfires'. A model of Guy Fawkes is placed on the bonfire, and fireworks are set off in celebration. Bonfire Night remains popular today largely because it is a time when families and friends can get together to celebrate.

**D**

However, as well as being a time for celebration, Bonfire Night also has wider social and political significance. It reminds people of the importance of the leaders of the country for stability, and the role of the law that protects us. Moreover, Bonfire Night reminds us that change should not occur through violence, an important message in this time of global terrorism.

**E**

As we have seen, Bonfire Night has a long history. However, I believe that many people have forgotten the historical significance of the story and just want to celebrate and enjoy the festival. Perhaps it is now just as important as a community event in the middle of winter when Christmas seems a long way ahead.

> **express tip**
>
> Don't spend too much time giving descriptive detail in Task 2 essays; focus mainly on analysing the issue and supporting your own opinion with reasons.

**B** Look at the question exam in 2B again. Did the writer answer all the points in the question? Discuss with a partner.

## 4 Introducing and concluding your essay

> **express tip**
>
> Do not use too many words from the exam question in your introduction. Make sure you use your own words as much as possible.

**A** Look at the exam question below. Then read the three introductions (1–3). Which introduction do you think is the most effective? Discuss your ideas with a partner.

> *It is often argued that our family is the most important thing in our lives. Why is our family so important? Which other people in our lives are important to us? Why?*

1   Although every family is different and no family is perfect, it is generally agreed that family is central to the lives of many people no matter how old we are. In this essay I will explain why this is the case and then suggest other people who may influence and affect us.

**2** It is often argued that family is the most important thing in our lives. I will write about the reasons why family is so important and mention some other people who are important to us.

**3** I agree that family is very important. My uncle is very important to me because he looked after me when I was young. In this essay I will describe my uncle and what he did for me.

**B** You will also need to make sure you summarise your viewpoint in a conclusion. With a partner, look at these example conclusions to the same essay question and decide which you think is the most effective.

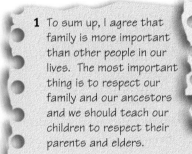

**1** To sum up, I agree that family is more important than other people in our lives. The most important thing is to respect our family and our ancestors and we should teach our children to respect their parents and elders.

**2** In conclusion, it is clear that our family is important as a result of the special bond in a 'blood' relationship and also because families form the basis of the societies in which we live. We have seen that other people can be equally important in our lives, though this depends on personal circumstances. In my case, my family has had a major and positive influence on my life and will always be important to me.

**3** In summary, I think it is obvious that family is the most important thing in our lives.

> **express tip**
>
> In your conclusion, you should quickly review your main idea(s), and then end with your overall opinion.

**C** Each example above starts with a useful phrase for beginning conclusions in Task 2 essays. Underline the phrases.

**D** Now write an introduction and a conclusion for the essay about an important festival in your country. Swap with a partner, and check your partner's writing for spelling, punctuation and grammatical errors.

## 5 General Training Writing Task 2: Essay

**for this task**

▸ Remember that for Writing Task 2 you only have about 40 minutes in total.

▸ Analyse the question carefully and underline the keywords. Decide what approach you need to take in answering the question (see also Units 4 and 8).

▸ Brainstorm ideas and relevant words and phrases, and then choose which ones you have time to include. Make sure you can cover all parts of the question.

▸ Decide how to structure your essay, and which points you will include in each paragraph. Don't use headings or bullet points. Use 2–3 paragraphs for the main part of your essay, plus an introduction and a conclusion.

▸ Make sure you answer the question fully, e.g. don't give too much descriptive detail if the question is asking you why you think something is true. Don't spend too long writing your introduction and conclusion, just use two or three sentences for each.

▸ Use the introduction to outline your approach to the whole essay, not just one part of it. In your conclusion, give an overall analysis (e.g. by referring back to one or two key arguments you made in the essay) with your personal opinion.

▸ Make sure you allow yourself a few minutes at the end to check your spelling, punctuation and grammar.

You should spend about 40 minutes on this task.

Write about the following topic.

> *Many people say we have a responsibility to look after the elderly people in our family or community. Why is it important to take care of them? How should we take care of them?*

Give reasons for your answer and include any relevant examples from your own knowledge or experience. Write at least 250 words.

### Questions 1–10

#### Questions 1–7
Complete the notes below.
Write **NO MORE THAN THREE WORDS AND/OR A NUMBER** for each answer.

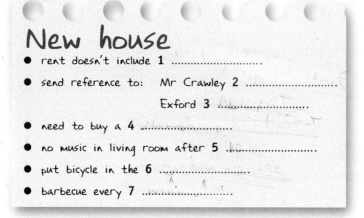

New house
- rent doesn't include **1** ........................
- send reference to:  Mr Crawley **2** ........................
  Exford **3** ........................
- need to buy a **4** ........................
- no music in living room after **5** ........................
- put bicycle in the **6** ........................
- barbecue every **7** ........................

#### Questions 8–10
Label the map below.
Write the correct letter **A–G** next to questions 8–10.

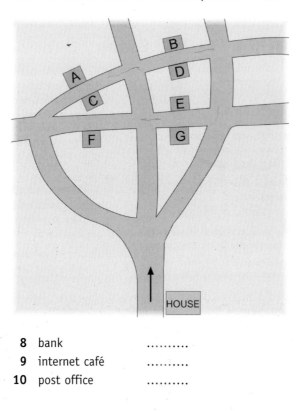

| | |
|---|---|
| **8** bank | .......... |
| **9** internet café | .......... |
| **10** post office | .......... |

## Questions 11–20

### Questions 11–16
Choose the correct letter, **A**, **B** or **C**.

11  The Apollo Leisure Centre opened in
   **A**  2000.
   **B**  2001.
   **C**  2002.

12  Which chart shows the different types of members currently?

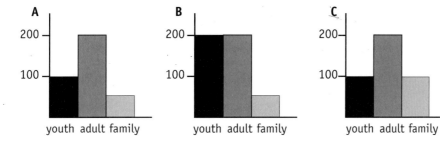

13  Which facility is planned for next year?
   **A**  swimming pool
   **B**  rock climbing wall
   **C**  massage room

14  Which type of membership is the best value for money?
   **A**  red
   **B**  green
   **C**  blue

15  When does the café close?
   **A**  8.00
   **B**  8.30
   **C**  9.00

16  How long is a typical consultation with the personal trainer?
   **A**  45 minutes
   **B**  1 hour
   **C**  1 hour 15 minutes

### Questions 17–20
Complete the timetable below.

| Monday | Class title |
| --- | --- |
| 4.00 – 5.00 | 17 ........................................ |
| 5.00 – 6.00 | 18 ........................................ |
| 6.15 – 7.30 | 19 ........................................ |
| 7.45 – 9.15 | 20 ........................................ |

### Questions 21–30

#### Questions 21–23

Complete the sentences below.

Write **NO MORE THAN TWO WORDS** for each answer.

**21**  Interviewing people was sometimes difficult because of the ............................. .

**22**  Aldo needs to talk to more ..................................... .

**23**  Dr Hurst advises Aldo to go to a ...................................... .

#### Questions 24 and 25

Choose **TWO** letters **A–F**.

Which **TWO** things do local people like in the area?

| | |
|---|---|
| **A** | cleaning services |
| **B** | colleges |
| **C** | parks |
| **D** | primary schools |
| **E** | sports facilities |
| **F** | street lighting |

**24** ..........

**25** ..........

#### Questions 26–30

Complete the table below.

Write **NO MORE THAN THREE WORDS** for each answer.

### Local festival

| Event | Location | Opportunity |
|---|---|---|
| Dance show | **26** ........................... | to observe different **27** ............................ |
| **28** ........................ | **29** ........................... | to learn about different cultures |
| Courses fair | Langtree Theatre | to interview the **30** ........................... |

## Questions 31–40

### Questions 31–34
Choose the correct letter, **A**, **B** or **C**.

31  The speaker agrees that cars are helpful for
    A    going to remote places.
    B    carrying large items.
    C    families travelling together.

32  According to the speaker, what advantage does road freight have over rail freight?
    A    It is more flexible.
    B    It is cheaper.
    C    It is more reliable.

33  Vehicle density is highest in
    A    Germany.
    B    the Netherlands.
    C    the UK.

34  A recent survey of bus passengers showed that the most common complaints concerned
    A    security.
    B    prices.
    C    timetabling.

### Questions 35–40
Complete the summary below.
Write **NO MORE THAN TWO WORDS** for each answer.

## Developments in public transport

Several steps are making public transport more attractive for users. These include introducing **35** ........ , which reduce the need for queueing. Schedules are being controlled with **36** ........ to increase efficiency. Also, buses are being made more **37**........ , and passengers are being given more **38**......... . Measures are being taken to create more flexibility for **39**........ travel. Transit companies have also benefited from different attitudes to **40** ......... . Together, these steps should increase public transport use.

*You should spend about 20 minutes on **Questions 1–13** which are based on Reading Passage 1 on pages 88 and 89.*

# WATER ON TAP

**A** Early people had no need for engineering works to supply their water. Hunters and nomads camped near natural sources and populations were so sparse that pollution of the water supply did not pose a serious problem. But as civilised life developed and small settlements grew into cities, water management became a major concern, not only to supply the urban centres but also to irrigate the farms surrounding them. The solution was to find a way to raise water up from the rivers.

**B** Around 5000 BC, primitive attempts were made by the Egyptians. They used the Perian Wheel, a water-wheel that dipped containers into a river, lifting up water as it revolved. Another method was a simple lever-and-bucket system called the shadoof. The invention of the lever, as well as a screw, to lift water is often attributed to Archimedes (287–213 BC) but both devices were without doubt in use thousands of years before his time. A more accurate explanation is that Archimedes was the first to try to describe in mathematical terms the way these devices worked.

**C** By 2000 BC, the rulers of Mesopotamia, Babylonia and Egypt had constructed systems of dams and canals to control the flood waters of the Tigris, Euphrates and the Nile. Such canals not only irrigated crops but also supplied water for domestic purposes, the water being stored in large pottery jars, hand-carried from the river by household slaves. The remains of the earliest aqueduct on record have been pinpointed to the works of the Assyrian king and master builder Sennacherib (705–681 BC), who developed a 10-mile canal in three stages, including 18 fresh-water courses from the mountains.

**D** But we can thank the Romans for being the first to consider seriously the sanitation of their water supply. Faced with the problem of directing enough water towards Rome — water from the Tiber, a muddy, smelly river, was out of the question — they set about constructing the most extensive system of aqueducts in the ancient world. These brought the pure waters of the Apennine Mountains into the city, with settling basins and filters along the way, to ensure the water's clarity and cleanliness. The first, built around 312 BC during Appius Claudius Caecus's administration, was Aqua Appia, an underground aqueduct about 10 miles in length.

**E** The arch revolutionised water supply.

By using it, Roman architects could raise aqueducts to the height needed to span valleys. The Aqua Marcian in Rome – around 56 miles long with a 10-mile bridged section – was built by the praetor Marcius in 144 BC, and was the first to carry water above ground. Eventually, Rome was served by eleven linked aqueducts. These kept the city's taps and fountains running – providing an astonishing 38 million gallons of water each day. Parts of several of these are still in use, although the construction of such massive water-supply systems declined with the fall of the Roman Empire. For several centuries afterwards, springs and wells provided the main source of domestic and industrial water.

F The introduction of the force pump in England in the middle of the 16th century greatly extended the possibilities of development of water-supply systems. This pump was by no means a new invention. It was in fact the brainchild of Ctesibius of Alexandria and it dates to the 3rd century BC. Like all great engineers, Ctesibius took his inspiration from his surroundings. While working on a way to raise and lower a mirror in his father's barber shop by counterbalancing it with a lead weight, he stumbled on a method of automatically closing the shop's door without it slamming. He ran a weighted line from the door over a pulley and into a pipe, which slowed the speed at which the weight dropped. As the door hissed away, opening and closing, he realised the weight was displacing air and acting as a piston. This realisation led Ctesibius to investigate methods of moving fluids along a pipe using a piston, and to the founding principle of hydraulics. Ctesibius's force pump was not capable of pumping high volumes of water but it played a vital part in ancient Greek culture. Among other uses, force pumps drained the bilges of the trading ships of the time. They were used to extinguish fires and they brought to life the fountains that graced Alexandria.

G In London, the first pumping waterworks were completed in 1562. This pumped river water to a reservoir suspended 120ft above the Thames. It was then distributed by gravity via lead pipes to surrounding buildings. In more recent times, many aqueducts have been built worldwide. Among them are the aqueducts supplying water to Glasgow (35 miles long), Marseilles (60 miles), Manchester (96 miles), Liverpool (68 miles) and Vienna (144 miles). California now has the most extensive aqueduct system in the world. Water drawn from the Colorado River's Parker Dam is carried 242 miles over the San Bernadino Mountains, supplying more than a billion gallons a day. In addition, the 338-mile Los Angeles aqueduct draws water from the Owens River in the Sierra Nevada, giving a daily supply of around 4 billion gallons.

### Questions 1–6

Complete the table below.

Choose **NO MORE THAN THREE WORDS** from the passage for each answer.

Write your answers in boxes 1–6 on your answer sheet.

| EGYPTIANS (5000 BC) | MESOPOTAMIA, BABYLONIA & EGYPT (2000 BC) | ROMANS | ENGLAND |
|---|---|---|---|
| • Perian Wheel (a type of water-wheel)<br><br>• **1** ........ (a lever and bucket system) | • systems of dams and canals<br><br>• water for **2** ........ and ........<br><br>• **3** ........ used for keeping water in | • dealt with water supply **4** ........<br><br>• system of aqueducts<br><br>• invention of **5** ........ led to aqueducts above ground | • use of force pump<br><br>• water pumped to reservoir and carried to buildings through **6** ........ |

### Questions 7–10

Reading Passage 1 has seven paragraphs labelled **A–G**.

Which paragraph contains the following information?

Write the correct letter **A–G** in boxes 7–10 on your answer sheet.

7   an invention that could only supply limited amounts of water
8   a reference to a widespread but false belief
9   reasons why water-supply systems needed to be developed
10   the name of the person responsible for creating the first known aqueduct

### Questions 11–13

Answer the questions below using **NO MORE THAN THREE WORDS** for each answer.

Write your answers in boxes 11–13 on your answer sheet.

11   What was Ctesibius trying to move?
12   What did Ctesibius succeed in causing to move?
13   What area of science did Ctesibius help to establish?

### Questions 14–26

*You should spend about 20 minutes on **Questions 14–26** which are based on Reading Passage 2 on the following pages.*

### Questions 14–19

*Reading Passage 2 has six paragraphs **A–F**.*

*Choose the correct heading for each paragraph from the list of headings below.*

*Write the correct numbers **i–x** in boxes 14–19 on your answer sheet.*

---

**List of Headings**

| | |
|---|---|
| **i** | Predictable behaviour |
| **ii** | Interpreting evidence |
| **iii** | An out-of-date image of wolves |
| **iv** | New problems for wolves |
| **v** | Preventing negative views of wolves |
| **vi** | Wolves who may be sheltering |
| **vii** | Understandable reactions |
| **viii** | Contrasting behaviour patterns among wolves |
| **ix** | A largely unnoticed increase |
| **x** | Damage done by wolves |

---

**14** Paragraph **A**

**15** Paragraph **B**

**16** Paragraph **C**

**17** Paragraph **D**

**18** Paragraph **E**

**19** Paragraph **F**

# HOWL OF WOLVES NEARS US SUBURBS

**A** Phil Miller flies the single-engine plane in a tight circle at an altitude of about 300 feet, listening on his headset to beeping from a wolf's radio collar. The animal is somewhere below, in a mix of patchy pine forest and low, sparse brush scattered over a snow-covered swamp. It is a gray day, drizzling and misty, and after the plane circles a line of pines several times, the wolf is still not visible. Then Mr Miller spots a pair – their coats a peppery mix of gray, black and cinnamon – standing casually under a pine tree, looking for all the world like they are trying to decide whether it's worth going out in the rain. If they were really worried about the weather, they might go to the vast Mall of America in Bloomington, Minnesota, only a two-hour drive away – or a 190-kilometer trot, no great challenge for a wolf. These wolves are not on Arctic tundra or in the confines of Yellowstone National Park. They are in Wisconsin, not exactly the suburbs, but not the wilderness either.

**B** In their quiet way they have shown that wolves do not need pristine wilderness to be successful, that they do not necessarily need a highly managed reintroduction programme, as used in Yellowstone, and that they can increase their range without stirring conflict among wolf proponents and opponents. 'Once wolves were thought emblematic of wilderness,' said Dr Adrian Treves, a biologist with the Wildlife Conservation Society in New York who has just published an analysis of what conditions are most likely to bring wolves and people into conflict. But the nearly 350 wolves of Wisconsin, in 80 known packs, have shown that they can cope with people.

**C** 'The wolves,' Dr Treves said, 'have managed to make dens and breed successfully for 25 years on a lot of private land, on county and state forest land, which is heavily, heavily used by recreationalists like snowmobilers, cross-country skiers and hunters. This is the classic case of the quiet recovery of wolves without a big fanfare, without big attention.' He added that because the wolves conducted their own repopulation, public reaction had been largely favourable. In the 1950s, northern Minnesota had a remnant population of a few hundred wolves, Dr Treves said. After the Endangered Species Act was passed in 1973, the protection it afforded, along with some forest regeneration and a change in attitudes, allowed the wolves to start growing in number. There are now more than 3,000 wolves in Minnesota, Michigan and Wisconsin.

**D** The day after flying with Mr Miller, who tracks wolves from the air, I went with Adrian Wydeven as he drove slowly around on sandy roads looking for wolf tracks in the same forested areas. Mr Wydeven, a mammalian ecologist, has been in charge of the wolf programme for the Wisconsin Department of Natural Resources for about 10 years. The talking stopped when we saw tracks in the sand. These were wolf tracks, not the large dog tracks we had seen earlier. 'If you look at these tracks,' he said, 'they're more elongated than those other tracks.' He noted that the wolf was not trotting but running, so that both back feet set down at once and then both front feet – a gallop. 'If he's chasing after a deer, that would make sense,' Mr Wydeven said. Stepping into the snow at the side of the road, he added, 'It looks like the deer veers off a bit here.' The tracks were fresh. 'I would say less than a day. I would say a few hours. It could be this morning. There might be just a pair.'

**E** The road is just a few miles from a cattle operation that has claimed significant depredations from wolves each year. Those attacks on livestock are the central problem in any resurgence of predators, and it is those attacks that Dr Treves has been studying. The state compensates anyone who has suffered loss from wolves. The highest risk, Dr Treves said, was 'at the colonization front' where an expanding wolf population, especially young, inexperienced wolves, comes into contact with people who are unused to coping with wolves.

**F**  His findings may lead wildlife managers away from lethal control, which Dr Treves said is inefficient at getting the wolves that are preying on livestock. The more refined the understanding of how wolves and people interact, the better the chances are for keeping the public on the side of the wolves. The wolves are doing their part to keep their population growing. When Mr Wydeven was inspecting the tracks in the road, we came on a spot where the road was all scuffed up with tracks. 'They're milling about here,' he said. I asked whether they might be playing. 'They might be, or they might be mating,' he replied. 'We're still in the breeding season.'

From "Howl of Wolves Nears U.S. Suburbs," by James Gorman. Copyright © 2004 by the New York Times Co.

## Questions 20–23

Complete the notes below.

Choose **NO MORE THAN THREE WORDS** from the passage for each answer.

Write your answers in boxes 20–23 on your answer sheet.

## Wolves in the US

- may not require an organised **20** ........... , as carried out in one of the national parks

- have reproduced for some time on land used by **21** ........... of various kinds

- greatest danger of wolves attacking is at a place known as **22** ...........

- a policy of **23** ........... may not prevent attacks on cattle

## Questions 24–26

Choose **THREE** letters **A–F**.

Write your answers in boxes 24–26 on your answer sheet.

Which **THREE** of the following are mentioned as new developments concerning wolves in the US?

    **A**    the places they now inhabit

    **B**    their ability to adapt to climate changes

    **C**    a change from living in packs to living in smaller groups

    **D**    their ability to coexist with people

    **E**    the fact that they have benefited from environmental initiatives

    **F**    a change in their behaviour towards other animals

You should spend about 20 minutes on **Questions 27–40** which are based on Reading Passage 3 on pages 94 and 95.

# MISSION OUT OF CONTROL

*It's not just physical dangers astronauts have to contend with —*
*psychological friction is a big problem, says Raj Persaud*

On space missions, weightlessness and radiation are often seen as being the key dangers. But there is increasing evidence to show that one of the greatest hazards lies in the crew itself. The hostile space environments and the hardware are, of course, crucial factors in any space mission. But so is the software of the human brain.

During long missions, space travellers have shown signs of increased territoriality, withdrawal and need for privacy. As a result of these sorts of psychological difficulties, one cosmonaut had a religious experience that led him to make a dangerous, unauthorised spacewalk. Nasa's Skylab missions in 1973 and 1974 almost immediately ran into trouble. One astronaut erroneously changed the control systems while suffering from psychological problems. Crew members began the third mission with a schedule that was too strenuous. They fell behind in their work and became demoralised. On their 45th day in space, the crew went on strike, refusing to perform scheduled tasks. Disregarding orders was an unusual and dangerous response for astronauts. After concessions from mission control, the crew settled down and eventually completed an 84-day mission.

The Russians have identified three phases in adaptation to space. The first lasts up to two months and is dominated by adjustments to the new environment. This is followed by increasing fatigue and decreasing motivation, 'asthenia'. What once seemed exciting becomes boring and repetitive. Next comes a lengthy period during which the asthenia, which can include depression and anxiety, worsens. The spacefarers are unusually upset by loud noises or unexpected information. This is the period when crew members get testy with one another and with the ground crew. There have been reports describing how one crew member did not speak to another for days; there are even rumours of fist fights — one over a chess game. Tensions frequently spill over to mission control, as they did in the Skylab strike. One Russian crew aboard a Salyut space station reportedly got so cross with mission control that they shut down communications for 24 hours.

According to Henry Cooper, who wrote a book, *A House in Space*, on the loneliness of the long-distance astronaut, at least three missions have been aborted for reasons that were in part psychological. In the 1976 Soyuz-21 mission to the Salyut-5 space station, the crew was brought home early after the cosmonauts complained fiercely of an acrid odour in the space station's environmental control system. No cause was ever found, nor did other crews smell it; conceivably, it was a hallucination. Coincidentally, the crew had not been getting along. The crew of the Soyuz T-14 mission to Salyut-7 in 1985 was brought home after 65 days after Vladimir Vasyutin complained that he had a prostate infection. Later, the doctors believed that the problem was partly psychological. Vasyutin had been getting behind in his work and was under pressure, having been passed over for a flight several times before. Alexander Laveikin returned early from the Soyuz TM-2 mission to the Mir space station in 1987 because he complained of a cardiac irregularity. Flight surgeons could find no sign of it. The cosmonaut had been under stress – he had made a couple of potentially serious errors. And he had not been getting along with his partner, Yuri Romanenko.

The same psychological phenomena curse men and women on expeditions to remote places. Isolation and sensory deprivation are the common denominators, whether the mission is in the Arctic wastes or the realm of the deep, causing a series of symptoms – heightened anxiety, boredom, depression, loneliness, excessive fear of danger and homesickness. The scientists and support staff who work in Antarctica have been studied by Dr Joanna Wood of the National Space Biomedical Research Institute in Houston, who also studies how crews behave in a special test chamber. 'After a few months, you get tired of looking at the same faces. People frequently have behaviours that might be endearing in the larger society, but when you're living with it day after day it's an annoyance.'

This continent, the last to be explored by humans, is the coldest, windiest and driest land mass. Because of the extreme environment, researchers must 'winter over' for six months out of the year. During this period, there is little contact with the outside world and groups tend to be confined indoors by the extreme temperatures. Antarctica has served as one of the primary means of gathering psychosocial data for space missions, according to Dr John Annexstad, a space scientist and ten-time veteran of scientific missions to Antarctica.

During the first few months of an Antarctic mission, interpersonal problems don't play a major part. The problem arises, says Dr Annexstad, after the initial shock and awe of the environment wear off, and crew members get to know their surroundings a little better. Then they begin to rebel against authority and each other. In one ice base, anxiety episodes increased from 3 during the first four months to 19 during the last four. In a study of personnel who wintered over in the Antarctic, 85 per cent reported periods of significant depression, 65 per cent had periods of anger or hostility, 60 per cent suffered from sleep disturbance, and 53 per cent had impaired cognition. During the 1977 International Biomedical Expedition to Antarctica, a 12-man adventure lasting 72 days, bickering became such a problem that psychologists accompanying the expedition had to intervene. Antarctic literature is full of stories about teammates who stopped talking to one another or even fought – one concerns a cook with a meat cleaver facing off against an engineer brandishing a fire axe.

**Questions 27–29**

Complete the sentences below with words taken from Reading Passage 3.

Use **NO MORE THAN THREE WORDS** for each answer.

Write your answers in boxes 27–29 on your answer sheet.

27  Space travellers on long missions demonstrate the desire to have some ............ .

28  Astronauts can get into a state called ............ after two months in space.

29  The causes of psychological problems on both space missions and expeditions to remote places are ............ together with ............ .

**Questions 30–35**

Look at the statements (**Questions 30–35**) and the list of space missions below.

Match each statement with the space mission it refers to.

Write the correct letter **A–D** in boxes 30–35 on your answer sheet.

**NB** You may use any letter more than once.

30  Two of the astronauts had a bad relationship with each other.

31  The astronauts decided not to carry out their duties.

32  One of the astronauts did not complete the mission.

33  One of the astronauts had failed to be selected for previous missions.

34  One of the astronauts made a mistake with the equipment.

35  The astronauts perceived something that may not have existed.

| List of Space Missions |
|---|
| **A**  Skylab |
| **B**  Soyuz-21 |
| **C**  Soyuz T-14 |
| **D**  Soyuz TM-2 |

**Questions 36–40**

Complete the summary below using words from the box.

Write your answers in boxes 36–40 on your answer sheet.

## Antarctic missions

According to Dr John Annexstad, relationships are not an important factor during the first part of a mission because crew members lack **36** ............ with their environment and have a feeling of **37** ............. . After this, there is less **38** ............ from crew members and the number of events caused by **39** ............ increases enormously as the mission continues. According to some stories, relationships can even result in **40** ............ involving crew members.

| | | | |
|---|---|---|---|
| expectation | boredom | cooperation | improvement |
| sympathy | discussion | familiarity | error |
| determination | carelessness | disappointment | violence |
| amazement | involvement | misunderstanding | confidence |
| failure | tension | competition | envy |

▶ WRITING TASK 1

You should spend about 20 minutes on this task.

*The table below gives information about online shopping in one year in the UK. It shows the amounts of money spent on various items by men and women and the percentages for men and women of the total money spent on those items.*

*Write a report for a university lecturer describing the information below.*

Write at least 150 words.

## ONLINE SHOPPING

|  | Expenditure (£m) | | | Share of market (%) | |
|---|---|---|---|---|---|
|  | Men | Women | Total | Men | Women |
| Grocery | 340.1 | 762.9 | 1103 | 30.8 | 69.2 |
| Furniture and floor coverings | 56.5 | 123.5 | 180 | 31.4 | 68.6 |
| Health and beauty | 40.2 | 81.8 | 122 | 33.0 | 67.0 |
| Clothing and footwear | 176.8 | 348.2 | 525 | 33.7 | 66.3 |
| Homewares | 85.4 | 120.6 | 206 | 41.5 | 58.5 |
| Books | 168.5 | 201.5 | 370 | 45.5 | 54.5 |
| Electrical goods | 829.6 | 324.4 | 1154 | 71.9 | 28.1 |
| DIY goods | 259.7 | 90.3 | 350 | 74.2 | 25.8 |
| Music and video | 280.0 | 148.0 | 428 | 65.4 | 34.6 |
| Other | 242.1 | 187.9 | 430 | 56.3 | 43.7 |
| Total | 2479 | 2389 | 4868 | 50.9 | 49.1 |

You should spend about 40 minutes on this task.

Present a written argument or case to an educated reader with no specialist knowledge of the following topic.

> **These days it is neither possible nor desirable for most people to stay in the same job throughout their working lives.**
> **To what extent do you agree or disagree with this statement?**

You should use your own ideas, knowledge and experience and support your arguments with examples and relevant evidence.

Write at least 250 words.

**PART 1**

**Example questions**

- Where do you live?
- What kind of place is it?
- What do you like best about where you live?
- What kinds of jobs do people do where you live?
- Would you say it is a good place to work in?

- How much time do you spend playing or watching sports?
- Which sports are most popular in your country?
- Which sports did you do when you were at school?
- Do you think all children should do some sport?

- Do you like cooking?
- How often do you go to restaurants?
- What kinds of restaurants do you enjoy eating in?
- What does a restaurant need to do to be successful?

**PART 2**

**Example task**

Read the topic card below carefully.

You will have to talk about the topic for one to two minutes.

You have one minute to think about what you are going to say.

You can make notes if you want.

> **Describe a shop that you enjoy going to.**
> **You should say:**
>     **where this shop is**
>     **what it sells**
>     **how often you go there**
> **and explain why you enjoy visiting this shop.**

**PART 3**

**Example questions**

- Are there certain kinds of shops that are becoming more popular?
- What disadvantages do you think there may be to an increase in consumerism?
- In what ways do you think advertising affects people's attitudes?
- In what ways do you think shopping may change in the future?

### Questions 1–14

#### Questions 1–7

Read the local council leaflet about recycling on the following page.

Complete each sentence with the correct ending **A–J** from the box below.

Write the correct letter **A–J** in boxes 1–7 on your answer sheet.

1   By phoning 020 8371 3670, you can find out about services that

2   The bring banks provided by the council

3   It is possible that certain bring banks

4   The terms of the Compost at Home scheme

5   The containers at the Summers Lane site

6   The details of the Summers Lane site

7   Visits to the Summers Lane site in large vehicles

---

**A**   require an arrangement to be made in advance.

**B**   mean that residents can buy equipment at a reduced cost.

**C**   have been changed recently.

**D**   are situated in various locations in the area.

**E**   are not available to local residents.

**F**   involve residents leaving things out for collection.

**G**   include a request that people organise items themselves.

**H**   will accept a greater range of items than others.

**I**   may be discontinued in the future.

**J**   are not only for things that can be recycled.

---

# RECYCLING
### *SO SIMPLE, IT'S EASY!*

## Here's How ...

**Recycle from Home:**

is an easy-to-use weekly service for local residents that collects batteries (household and car), cans, engine oil, foil, glass, mobile phones, paper, shoes, textiles and yellow pages from your doorstep. For further information, contact ECT Recycling:

020 8371 3670 / info@ECTrecycling.co.uk *quoting ref: RH 1DL*

**Bring Banks:**

The council has many bring banks in the borough. They can take some or all of the following materials: books, cans, glass, paper, shoes and textiles.

For more information call: 020 8359 4654 *quoting ref: BB 1DL*

**Flats Recycling Service:**

is an easy-to-use free weekly service for all local residents living in flats. Recycling bins are installed to enable residents to recycle cans, glass and paper.

To find out more, contact ECT Recycling: 020 8371 3670/ info@ECTrecycling.co.uk
*quoting ref: FR 1DL*

**Compost at Home:**

Home composting can reduce the rubbish in your household's bin by one third and create free compost! The council is helping to minimise waste by offering residents the opportunity to purchase home composters at subsidised prices. Anyone can take part and you do not need to be a keen gardener or have a big garden to make compost.

For further information telephone: 020 8359 4654 and request a leaflet/order form
*quoting ref: COMP 1DL*

**Civic Amenity and Recycling Centre:**

is based at Summers Lane. At the site you can recycle and dispose of a wide range of goods including: batteries (household and car), books, cardboard, fridges, furniture, gas bottles, garden waste, paint, plastic bottles, scrap metal, tyres and wood. Where possible please sort your waste into the above categories. The site is open Monday to Saturday 8 am to 4 pm and Sundays and Bank Holidays 9 am to 4 pm. The site is closed Christmas Day, Boxing Day and New Year's Day. Residents bringing vans need to ring and make an appointment. The site does not accept commercial waste.

For more information contact the site on: 020 8362 0752 /info@ECTrecycling.co.uk
*quoting ref: CA 1DL*

*Questions 8–14*

*Read the museum information below.*

*Complete the sentences below with words taken from the passage.*

*Write **NO MORE THAN TWO WORDS** for each answer.*

*Write your answers in boxes 8–14 on your answer sheet.*

8   Visitors can find out how well-directed their .............. are.

9   After running in a race, visitors can see an .............. of it.

10   Visitors who don't want to take part in physical activities can learn about incredible .............. in sport.

11   Visitors can learn about the relationship between how tall they are and their .............. .

12   Visitors can learn about the effect that wearing the right .............. might have.

13   The interactives enable visitors to assess their .............. in a variety of ways.

14   The merchandise includes .............. that cannot be purchased anywhere else.

## SCIENCE MUSEUM SPECIAL EXHIBITION
### SCIENCE OF SPORT

**SCIENCE OF SPORT** explains the science behind sport and encourages children (and adults!) to get themselves interacting with our state-of-the-art exhibits.

Instead of looking at displays, you'll actually be in them, taking part in races, games and quizzes to test your skills and knowledge of sport. And while you're playing, you're learning too!

Try out the interactive displays and simulated experiences – dribble a football against the clock, climb an indoor rock face, test the accuracy of your tennis shots, or compete against friends in a quick sprint complete with action replay! Compare your scores with those of your friends and family to see who comes out on top.

You don't have to be an avid sportsman or woman to enjoy this exhibition – you'll find it's just as much fun learning new activities or even discovering hidden talents! For those who prefer a less energetic visit, you can get a closer look at some of the amazing inventions in the sports world that have helped produce record-breaking competitors.

**SCIENCE OF SPORT** answers your questions about all sorts of topics – coordination, ability, diet, exercise and the technology of sport today all feature in this exhibition. Learn how your height influences your throwing abilities, why good reflexes improve your game or even how a good pair of trainers can help you run faster. With the aid of our interactives you can also learn more about your own fitness by checking your pulse, measuring how tall you are, weighing yourself and testing your reactions.

**The exhibition is open daily from 10.00 to 18.00.**

Merchandise including professional equipment, exclusive branded souvenirs and inspiring gifts, suitable for a range of ages, will be on sale in the accompanying exhibition store.

## Questions 15–27

### Questions 15–20

*Read the information below about student services at a college.*

*Answer the questions below USING NO MORE THAN THREE WORDS for each answer.*

*Write your answers in boxes 15–20 on your answer sheet.*

**15** Which individual can give students advice?

**16** Which eating place is said to be comparatively cheap?

**17** Which eating place may get full?

**18** Who is employed to make sure that everyone is safe?

**19** What does the college expect everyone to be?

**20** What does the college check to make sure nobody is treated unfairly?

# COLLEGE SERVICES FOR STUDENTS

*The following are among the services provided by the College.*

### STUDENT COMMON ROOM & GAMES ROOM

You can relax in the Student Common Room – there's music & TV and help available from our student services team, including the Youth Worker and Student Union Executives. On the other hand, you might want to let off steam in the Games Room with pool and table tennis.

### WHERE TO EAT

*The Refectory*
• everything from confectionery, a quick snack, hot and cold drinks to a full meal – all at the keenest prices. Open every day from 8.30 am.

*The Bistro*
• the very best of European snacks and light meals. 2nd floor of the main building. Open every day 10.00 am–3.00 pm.

*The Restaurant*
• for a really sophisticated dining experience, try either lunch (noon–2.00 pm) or dinner (7.00–10.00 pm) in our licensed restaurant. We recommend that you book in advance on 020 8982 5068.

*The Oaktree Café*
• snacks and drinks are available between 10.00 am and 3.00 pm with a full meal service at lunchtime.

### SECURITY

We are an open access college and we take your safety and security very seriously. In order to maintain a safe environment for everyone, we provide Student Identity Cards, which must be worn and be visible at all times. Our commitment to maintaining a safe and secure environment for our students, staff and visitors is supported by a security team and closely monitored Closed Circuit Television (CCTV).

### EQUAL OPPORTUNITIES

The College attracts students from a wide range of backgrounds and cultures. We work on the assumption that anyone entering the College shares our view that all people have a right to an education to meet their particular needs, in an atmosphere in which individuals are respected. We make every effort, therefore, to ensure that no one is treated unfavourably on grounds of race, gender, age or disability. We have an Equal Opportunities policy, monitor our enrolments and have firm rules dealing with racial and sexual harassment.

*Questions 21–27*

*Read the information below from a college prospectus.*

*Do the following statements agree with the information given in the passage?*

*In boxes 21–27 on your answer sheet write*

> **TRUE**        *if the statement agrees with the information*
>
> **FALSE**       *if the statement contradicts the information*
>
> **NOT GIVEN**  *if there is no information on this*

21   Entry requirements may differ on different courses.

22   Requirements for mature students have recently changed.

23   Acceptance on a course may depend on when the application is sent.

24   The Admissions Service will provide extra copies of the Application and Reference forms.

25   Course numbers are given for all courses.

26   Applicants should send their references to the Admissions Service.

27   A firm offer may be withdrawn after receipt of a reference.

## HOW TO APPLY FOR A COURSE AT THE COLLEGE

### COURSE ENTRY REQUIREMENTS

All full-programme applicants will be interviewed for their course. Students on ALL courses must be dedicated and prepared to work hard. See the individual course details in this prospectus for any specific admission requirements.

Students must be at least 16 years old, unless under an arrangement with their school. Mature students are encouraged to apply – if you don't have the formal entry requirements, you may be accepted on the basis of an interview.

### WHEN TO APPLY

Send us your application as soon as possible because some programmes fill up very quickly. Don't wait for your exam results! Priority for the programme originally applied for is based on the date the application is received. All applications should be received by 25 July. However, in some cases later applicants will be accepted.

### MAKING AN APPLICATION

Detach and complete the Application and Reference forms, which are at the back of this prospectus. Read the following notes before filling in your forms. Call the Admissions Service with any queries.

If a course number is given, please make sure you write it in the box provided on the application form. Course numbers are in the course pages of the prospectus, under the course title and next to the College Centre where the course is held.

### REFERENCE

Write your full name, address and the learning programmes you have chosen on your reference form and send it to someone who knows of your progress so far. This will usually be your present or last headteacher or tutor. For students over 20, we may accept a reference from someone who knows you well – for example an employer (not a relative). The suitability of your referee should be confirmed with the Admissions Service.

Ask the person providing your reference to return the form as soon as possible to the Admissions Service. You may not be offered an interview until a satisfactory reference form is received by the Admissions Officer. We cannot offer a firm place on a programme until a reference has been received.

## Questions 28–40

*Read the following passage and answer Questions 28–40.*

# NTROPY

**How a 20-year-old idea eventually became a moneyspinner**

**A** The story of how games designer Paul Wickens achieved success with his bestselling game Ntropy is an object lesson to those who want to strike out on their own. Firstly, there's no need to rush. 'I had the idea for what ended up as Ntropy – which, by the way, is a play on the word entropy, meaning chaos or disorganisation – about 20 years ago,' says Mr Wickens. 'I was building structures with matchsticks while waiting for some friends in a bar. Later I made a scaled-up version of a box of matches, which we used to play with at college for hours on end.'

**B** After leaving college, Mr Wickens, though interested in starting his own company and having designed another couple of games by then, took the safety-first route. 'I got a job in IT as a programmer,' he recalls. 'Later I moved into sales support in specific applications, mostly centred round e-commerce. For the most part I forgot about my games.' So what reawakened his interest? 'It was about two years ago,' says Mr Wickens, 'and there was a downturn in the IT industry. Several of my friends and even colleagues lost their jobs and a couple of them started their own companies. And yes, I suppose I did re-evaluate in the way you do when you think: "What would I do if I were made redundant?" '

**C** What most people don't do is try to crack the £2 billion-a-year UK toy and games market. 'I chose Ntropy,' he explains, 'because it involves all the family. I wrote to several of the big games companies with a brief outline of my game and received the polite "Thanks, but no thanks" reply.' It is at this point, says Mr Wickens, that he began to think seriously about going it alone as an independent. 'OK, I knew nothing about the UK toy market but I had a lot more general business experience than I did when I left college.'

**D** The next step was to make a full replica of the game, mostly in his workshop – a converted garage at home. 'Then I had to test it. My father helped here because he works at an outdoor centre. He gave it to people who had no idea who I was. I figured I had to get third parties to assess it and listen to what they had to say.' The result was a return to the workshop for 'a fairly drastic redesign and some rule changes.'

**E** Nevertheless, the designer was convinced by now that Ntropy had commercial potential. The next question was: 'Am I prepared to spend what it takes for the next stage of development?' On the money side, Mr Wickens says it represented his savings over 20 years and remortgaging his house. He set up a company, Tadpole Games – friends helped with the design and logo for the firm and the game box – and he registered with the UK Patent Office at a cost of £4,000.

**F** The next stage was to design the plastic base on which the stick structure could be built. Mr Wickens says: 'A friend came up with the design and a firm I found used this very futuristic process called Selective Laser Sintering to produce the first mould. I kept the different parts of the project separate to protect it.'

**G** Each Ntropy game consists of 64 identical

sticks. 'I could only have done this with the help of the Internet,' he says. 'I spent weekend after weekend looking for a sustainable source of timber. In the end I found a firm in southern Thailand which used wood from rubber trees and could do it for about 20p a stick. It was also through the Net that I learned about letters of credit and shipping cargo on boats.'

**H** After an anxious six-week wait, the container arrived. 'I think it was a shock to my neighbours,' says Mr Wickens. 'There were 700 boxes with 300,000 sticks. I checked some samples and they were the right size. I was overjoyed.' Too soon. 'Over the next few days I went through the other boxes and found around half of them weren't the exact size I needed. It's the first really big lesson I've learned. Never do a deal like this without going and checking it out first.'

**I** Mr Wickens formally launched Ntropy to the trade at the London Toy Fair. Then a stroke of luck, essential to all budding entrepreneurs, came his way. As he tells it: 'I gave the game to a friend who was meeting some mates in the pub. They played and really enjoyed it. My friend rang the next day to tell me and added: "Oh, by the way, they work at Hamleys." ' Hamleys is London's top toy shop. 'Then their boss rang me to say, despite one or two concerns, "We like it, so let's give it a go".' The rest, as they say, is history. Ntropy took off and the first batch of 2,500 moved fast.

**J** And the future? 'I've just taken on someone to develop the commercial side of Tadpole,' says Mr Wickens. 'If that works out, he will take a stake in the business. I want Ntropy to be a global product but I don't necessarily see myself as an out-and-out businessman. I already have another couple of games I'd like to develop.'

**Questions 28–34**

Complete the flow chart below.

Choose **NO MORE THAN THREE WORDS** from the passage for each answer.

Write your answers in boxes 28–34 on your answer sheet.

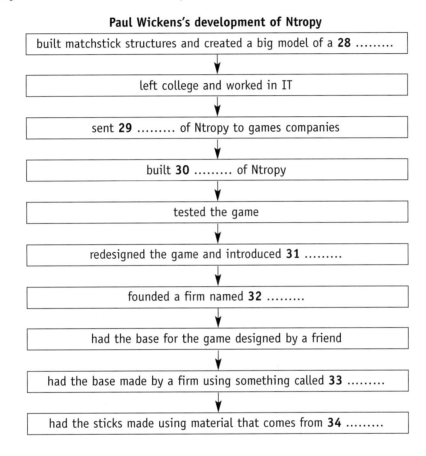

**Paul Wickens's development of Ntropy**

built matchstick structures and created a big model of a **28** .........

↓

left college and worked in IT

↓

sent **29** ......... of Ntropy to games companies

↓

built **30** ......... of Ntropy

↓

tested the game

↓

redesigned the game and introduced **31** .........

↓

founded a firm named **32** .........

↓

had the base for the game designed by a friend

↓

had the base made by a firm using something called **33** .........

↓

had the sticks made using material that comes from **34** .........

**Questions 35–40**

The passage has ten paragraphs labelled **A–J**.

Which paragraph contains the following information?

Write the correct letter **A–J** in boxes 35–40 on your answer sheet.

**35** a reference to an assumption Paul Wickens made that proved to be incorrect

**36** a reason why Paul Wickens thought he was qualified to start his own games company

**37** Paul Wickens's aim regarding the market for Ntropy

**38** a description of a coincidence that proved fortunate for Paul Wickens

**39** a reason why Paul Wickens began to consider his future

**40** an explanation of the name Paul Wickens gave to his game

**WRITING TASK 1**

You should spend about 20 minutes on this task.

> *You are currently taking a course at a college but you will need to have a week off during this course.*
>
> *Write a letter to the college Principal. In the letter*
>
> * *give details of your course*
> * *explain why you need a week off*
> * *say what you want the Principal to do.*

Write at least 150 words.

You do **NOT** need to write your own address.

Begin your letter as follows:

*Dear Sir/Madam,*

**WRITING TASK 2**

You should spend about 40 minutes on this task.
You have been asked to write about the following topic.

> *People shouldn't take as much interest as they do in the lives of celebrities and the gossip surrounding them.*
> *Do you agree or disagree?*

Give reasons for your answer and include any relevant examples from your experience.
Write at least 250 words.

# 1 Studying Overseas

## READING

### 2 Skimming and scanning

**A 1** scan; **2** scan; **3** skim; **4** skim

**B** 3

**C** over 70%: the amount of mail written in English; over 50%: the amount of business done in English

### 3 Predicting content

**A** 3

### 4 Short-answer questions

*Questions 1–5*
**1** (a) foundation course; **2** (the) British system; **3** liberty (and) freedom; **4** community college courses; **5** (the) United Nations

### 5 Classification

*Questions 6–10*
**6** US; **7** AU; **8** UK; **9** US; **10** NZ

### 6 True/False/Not Given

*Questions 11–15*
**11** False; **12** True; **13** True; **14** Not Given; **15** Not Given

## SPEAKING

### 2 Answering questions about yourself

**B 1** Do you enjoy studying English? **2** What do you do in your free time? **3** Do you plan to study abroad? **4** Do you have any brothers or sisters? **5** What's your job? **6** Where do you live?

**C a** I'm afraid; **b** It depends; **c** I guess; **d** Well; **e** In fact; **f** Actually

**D a** iii; **b** iv; **c** ii; **d** v; **e** i; **f** vi

### 3 Extending your responses

**D 1 Suggested keywords**
**1** good relationship, shared a room, argued, fight; **2** before that, studying in Ireland, for two years, living in countryside, get used to London eventually, takes time to adjust; **3** sports, team sports, cricket, baseball, soccer, football; **4** speaking with friends, reading, writing, vocabulary, learning, improve; **5** quit, working, nurse, dentist; **6** go to Sydney, study business, get a degree

### 2 Suggested follow-up questions

**1** How do you get on with your sister? What is your relationship like? Are you close?

**2** Where did you live before? How long did you live there? Did you like it? Do you like where you live now?

**3** What sports do you like? What sports would you like to play?

**4** What areas of English do you like? What is difficult? Are you happy with your progress?

**5** What did you use to do? How long did you do that job? What job would you like to do in the future? Why?

**6** Where do you want to go? What are you going to study? Why did you choose that country?

# 2 Shopping and the Internet

## LISTENING

### 1 Introduction

**A** mobile phone; **B** digital camera; **C** radio; **D** computer

### 2 Imagining the situation and language

**A** Topic related vocabulary may include: camera, digital, zoom, lens, pictures, photos and memory.

### 3 Identifying the question

**B 1** What is your name? **2** When were you born?/What is your date of birth? **3** How old are you? **4** Why are you taking IELTS?/Why do you want to take IELTS?

### 4 Identifying the answer type

**B 1** who; **2** how much; **3** which; **4** when; **5** where; **6** how many; **7** what percentage; **8** why

**C 1** name; **2** amount (of money); **3** name; **4** time; **5** place; **6** number; **7** percentage; **8** reason

**D 1** George; **2** 10/ten cents; **3** ABC; **4** (in the) evening(s); **5** newsagents and supermarkets; **6** 120; **7** 87%; **8** (much) safer

### 5 Form completion

**1** Banks; **2** 17A Leigham Street; **3** NT3 5OP; **4** 01382 25669; **5** banks123; **6** No

### 6 Notes completion

**1** green; **2** clock; **3** four/4; **4** 39.99; **5** TV;

**6** 100/(a/one) hundred; **7** Parker; **8** (the) Olympic; **9** solar; **10** 18

## WRITING

### 2 Understanding charts and tables

**A**

**Suggested answers**

**1** The title gives us an overview of the contents of the graph. **2** The vertical axis tells us what percentage of people use the Internet and shop online. **3** The horizontal axis gives us a breakdown of the different age groups surveyed. **4** The colour key tells us something about the respondents; in this case it differentiates between those using the Internet and those using it to shop.

**B 1** 65%; **2** 20%; **3** 5%

### 3 Describing general and specific information

**A 1** b; **2** e; **3** f; **4** c; **5** g; **6** a; **7** d

**B 1** b; **2** c; **3** b; **4** a; **5** c

### 4 Comparing and contrasting data

**A 1** Although/While; **2** However; **3** As well as, it also; **4** not only, but also

**B 1** more; **2** relatively small: **3** biggest; **4** music, computer software; **5** airline, entertainment; **6** slightly; **7** a great deal

### 5 Academic Writing Task 1: Report

A model answer is provided in the Teacher's Guide.

## 3 Jobs and Job-hunting

### READING

### 2 Identifying keywords and paraphrase

**A** The advertisement matches the picture of the journalist.

**B** Keywords: 'news channel', 'journalist', 'journalism'

**C 1** experienced; **2** initiative (to work independently); **3** fluent in

### 3 Matching information to sections of text

*Questions 1–4*
**1** B; **2** A; **3** D; **4** C

*Questions 5–10*
**5** C; **6** D; **7** A; **8** D; **9** A; **10** A

### 4 Table completion

*Questions 11–15*
**11** Yes; **12** 275; **13** (call) in person; **14** 16,525; **15** email

### 5 Sentence completion

*Questions 1–4*
**1** better-informed decision; **2** a good salary; **3** voluntary work; **4** a job advertisement

*Questions 5–8*
**5** E; **6** C; **7** A; **8** H

### SPEAKING

### 3 Organising your ideas

**A A** 2; **B** 3; **C** 1

**B A** Teacher: The student didn't talk about 'piano'.
**B** Chef: The student didn't talk about 'wedding parties'.
**C** Waitress: The student didn't talk about '3 months'.

## 4 Crime and Punishment

### LISTENING

### 1 Introduction

**A** murder; **B** smuggling; **C** arson; **D** burglary

### 2 Using keywords to predict the answer

**A 1** black

**B 2** (a) (client) report

**C 3** A
The question being asked here is 'Where was the briefcase stolen from'. It is important to underline 'dress' or 'dress-shop' and not just 'shop' because there is also a 'dry cleaner's shop'.

### 3 Identifying synonyms and paraphrase

**A 1** C
Ways of saying '12.00' include 'twelve o'clock', 'noon' and 'midday'. Ways of saying '1.45' include 'one forty-five', 'quarter to one' and 'quarter of one'. Ways of saying '2.15' include 'two fifteen', 'quarter past two' and 'a quarter after two'.

**B 2** (about) 5 minutes.
Synonyms for 'vehicle' include 'car', 'van', etc.

**C 3** A

**4 Multiple-choice questions; short-answer questions**

*Questions 1–5*

**1** A; **2** C; **3** B; **4** C; **5** C

*Questions 6–10*

**6** opposite the museum; **7** (loud) music; **8** white; **9** blue or green; **10** 0800 666 000

**5 Multiple-choice questions; notes completion**

*Questions 1–4*

**1** A; **2** B; **3** C; **4** A

*Questions 5–10*

**5** 40%; **6** older (cars); **7** car parks; **8** well-lit; **9** (the) keys; **10** can be seen

### WRITING

**2 Seeing two sides of an argument**

**A For:** 3, 4, 5; **Against:** 1, 2, 6

**3 Approaching the question**

**B 1** b; **2** d; **3** a; **4** c

**4 Organising your essay**

**A 1** C; **2** D; **3** A; **4** B

**B 1** b, f, i, r; **2** p; **3** e, g, o; **4** l, m; **5** h, k;
 **6** a, c, d, j, n, s; **7** q

**5 Academic and General Training: Essay**

A model essay is provided in the Teacher's Guide.

## 5 Transport and Inventions

### READING

**2 Building a mental map of the text**

**A i** 4; **ii** 1; **iii** 2; **iv** 3

**B 1** wings (for birdmen); **2** kites; **3** ornithopter;
 **4** hot air balloon; **5** glider; **6** propeller planes;
 **7** jet plane

**3 Rebuilding the text**

**A** Paragraph A: 3; Paragraph B: 2

**4 Matching headings to paragraphs**

**1** x; **2** vi; **3** viii; **4** vii; **5** ix; **6** iv; **7** i; **8** ii

**5 Multiple-choice questions**

**A 9** B

Keywords include 'Greek legend' and 'Icarus'.

You need to look at paragraph B.

**B 10** C; **11** D; **12** G; **13, 14** F

**C 10** D; **11** A; **12** D; **13, 14** C, E (in either order)

### SPEAKING

**2 Identifying types of questions**

**A 1** d; **2** c; **3** b; **4** a

**B i** 3; **ii** 1; **iii** 2; **iv** 4

**3 Giving an appropriate response**

**A 1** ii; **2** iv; **3** iii; **4** I

**C 1** Carlos; **2** Raj; **3** Li Lin

**4 Introducing and supporting an opinion**

**A 1** No cars in city centre; **2** Spend money on
 roads; **3** Speed limit is too low; **4** Drivers
 shouldn't pay higher taxes

**B 1** I think it'd be a good idea; Too much pollution
 **2** For me, ... is more important; People prefer
 cars; Example of uncomfortable trains in home
 country
 **3** I completely agree; Example of another country;
 **4** I tend to disagree; Logical explanation why
 higher taxes are unfair

## 6 The Natural World

### LISTENING

**2 Identifying attitude**

**A 1** d; **2** b; **3** c; **4** a

**B a** iii; **b** iv; **c** i; **d** ii

**C 1** iv; **2** i; **3** ii; **4** iii

**3 Identifying speakers**

**A** Cedric speaks six times.

**B 1** C; **2** C; **3** B; **4** A

**4 Classification**

**1** B; **2** B; **3** A; **4** C; **5** A; **6** C; **7** C

**5 Table completion; summary completion**

**A Questions 1–12**

**1** 250;  **2** Africa;  **3** two or more;  **4** zebra;
**5** females;  **6** nearly extinct;  **7** (work) in groups;
**8** 110;  **9** 6;  **10** Chile;  **11** forests;  **12** (their)
paws

**B Questions 1–6**

**1** oxygen;  **2** animals and plants;  **3** industrial;
**4** nests;  **5** pollution;  **6** chemicals

## WRITING

### 1 Introduction

**A** Left: New Delhi; top right: Singapore; bottom
right: Cairo

**B 1** The table represents rainfall in three cities over
the year; the line graph represents temperature in
three cities over the year.
**2** Temperature is measured in degrees Celsius;
rainfall is measured in millimetres.
**3** New Delhi has the highest temperature in a year.
Cairo has the lowest.
**4** Singapore has the highest rainfall in a year.
Cairo has the lowest.

### 2 Using the language of trends

**A 1** rise, increase ...;  **2** fall, drop ...;  **3** reach
a peak ...;  **4** fall to a low point ...;  **5** remain
stable ...;  **6** fluctuate, move up and down  ...;

**B** In Singapore, the amount of rainfall **drops
dramatically** from January to February. After a
**slight rise** in March, the level of rainfall
**decreases steadily** until July. Over the next three
months, the rainfall **fluctuates sharply**. Finally, at
the end of the year, we can see a **dramatic rise** in
rainfall in November and a **peak** in December.

In Cairo, the rainfall **remains constant** at 5mm
per month from January to March. It then
**declines gradually** to zero in July and August
before **rising gradually** again in the second half
of the year.

In New Delhi, there is a **steady drop** in rainfall
from January to March followed by a **dramatic
increase** to around 170–180 mm in July and
August. The final part of the year shows rainfall
**falling dramatically** to a **low point** of 3mm in
November.

**C 1** F;  **2** T;  **3** F

### 3 Describing trends

**A 1** very little;  **2** gradually;  **3** rising;  **4** fluctuates;

**5** sharp;  **6** reaching a peak;  **7** a low point;  **8** no
change;  **9** increase

**B 1** 'On the other hand';  **2** 'about', 'approximately'

**C 1** from, to, over;  **2** From, to, in;  **3** Between, of;
**4** by;  **5** in, in

### 4 Academic Writing Task 1: Report

A model answer is provided in the Teacher's Guide.

## 7 Food and Diet

### READING

### 2 Identifying opinions

**A i** No;  **ii** Yes;  **iii** Not Given

**B 1 i** No, **ii** Yes, **iii** Not Given;  **2 i** Not Given, **ii** No,
**iii** Yes

### 3 Yes/No/Not Given

**1** No;  **2** Yes;  **3** Not Given;  **4** Yes;  **5** Yes;
**6** Not Given;  **7** No;  **8** Yes

### 4 Summary completion

**B** Left to right, top to bottom: 4, 3, 1, 2

**Questions 9–15**

**9** agricultural productivity;  **10** public-health;
**11** safety and stability;  **12** behaviour;  **13** better
eating habits;  **14** (primary) school;  **15** comparable
countries

**Questions 16–19**

**16** society;  **17** government;  **18** levy;
**19** freedom

### SPEAKING

### 2 Describing an experience

**C 2** a, b, f, g and h
**3** Context: a, b; events: f;  feelings: h

### 4 Generating ideas

### C Example questions

Who is worried about fast food companies
advertising to children?

What kind of advertising might be acceptable?

Why should fast food companies limit their
advertising to children?

Where should fast food companies be able to freely
advertise?

When should fast food companies not advertise on TV?

How should advertising be controlled?

## 8 Sickness and Health

### LISTENING

#### 1 Introduction

A 1 treatment; 2 surgery; 3 cure; 4 administration; 5 architecture

#### 2 Understanding description

B 1 AB; 2 ICU; 3 OGU; 4 L; 5 FM

D 6 mental problems; 7 (medical) records; 8 surgery; 9 babies and children; 10 recovery

#### 3 Identifying differences between pictures

B 1 b

#### 4 Labelling a diagram

1 windpipe; 2 oxygen; 3 nutrients; 4 remove waste; 5 (kind of) bag

#### 5 Multiple-choice (pictures); multiple-choice with multiple answers

*Questions 1–2*
1 c; 2 a

*Questions 3–4*
3, 4 A, E (in either order)

### WRITING

#### 1 Introduction

A **Illness and cures:** die of cancer, get/have flu, get/have HIV/Aids, have an operation, take antibiotics, take medicine, undergo surgery
**Methods of prevention:** be a positive thinker, eat a balanced diet, get a vaccination, immunise against disease, reduce stress, sleep well, stop smoking, take up sport

#### 2 Supporting your statements and opinions

1 b; 2 a; 3 e; 4 c; 5 d

#### 4 Structuring an 'agree or disagree' essay

A Essay 1: agree; essay 2: disagree

C For both essays: 1 D; 2 C; 3 A; 4 B

D 1 To summarise, In conclusion; 2 ... so why

should society have to pick up the bill, Is it right ...? Who is going to play God ...? Who is going to decide...? 3 Do we refuse ...? Of course not. The government uses ... free health treatment? That is logical. 4 In Greece ... , 5 I don't think this argument is valid because ..., I disagree with this too, because ..., The problem with this argument ...; 6 I totally agree with the statement that ..., I completely disagree with the idea that ...

#### 5 Academic and General Training: Essay

A model essay is provided in the Teacher's Guide.

## General Training 1A

#### 2 Recognising types of letters

B 1 requesting information; 2 requesting a favour; 3 making a complaint; 4 explaining a situation; 5 introducing yourself

C 1 prospective student to school administration (formal); 2 classmate to classmate (informal); 3 customer to bank manager (formal); 4 student to school administration (formal); 5 student to host family (semi-formal)

D 1 a; 2 c; 3 e; 4 b; 5 d

#### 3 Planning a letter

A **Main purpose:** to request a loan; relationship: customer to bank manager; level of formality required: formal

C **Relevant points:** 1, 4, 5, 6, 7

D a: 1, 6; b: 4, 5; c: 7

#### 4 Using appropriate language and organisation

A Yes; Yes

B 5 has not been followed.

C 1 I would like to request; 2 Unfortunately, there has been an error; 3 I estimate that I will be able to; 4 Your assistance would be greatly appreciated; 5 I look forward very much to hearing from you soon

#### 5 General Training Writing Task 1: Letter

A model answer is provided in the Teacher's Guide.

## General Training 1B

### 2 Beginning a letter of complaint

**A 1** a hotel room; **2** a travel delay; **3** hotel staff

**B 1** package holiday company; **2** airline; **3** hotel

**C** Letter 2; 'I am writing to express my total dissatisfaction and frustration with ...'

### 3 Imagining the situation

**A** The purpose of the letter is to complain about a lack of heating and hot water. The relationship is tenant to landlord.

### 4 Describing past events

**B 1** since; **2** for two weeks; **3** Ten days ago; **4** two days; **5** After; **6** eventually; **7** five days later; **8** now; **9** immediately; **10** soon

### 5 Giving reasons for a complaint

**B** Indirect speech: He said he could not fix the problem because the water heater was too old. His exact words were possibly: 'I can't fix the problem because the water heater is too old.'

**C 1** You told us that you were a responsible landlord. **2** You said that you had just installed a new heating and hot water system. **3** You said that we were going to be very happy here. **4** You said that your workmen had always done an excellent job fixing any problems.

### 6 General Training Writing Task 1: Letter

A model answer is provided in the Teacher's Guide.

## General Training 2

### 2 Approaching the question

**A** 2; 3; 4; 5

**B** 3; 4; 5

### 3 Organising your essay

**A 1** C; **2** D; **3** A; **4** B; **5** E

### 4 Introducing and concluding your essay

**A** Introduction 1 is the most effective.

**B** Conclusion 2 is the most effective.

**C 1** To sum up; **2** In conclusion; **3** In summary

### 5 General Training Writing Task 2: Essay

A model essay is provided in the Teacher's Guide.

# 1 Studying Overseas

### 1.1

**1**

**A:** Do you enjoy studying English?

**B:** I'm afraid I don't like it very much. I think it's really difficult, especially the grammar.

**2**

**A:** What do you do in your free time?

**B:** It depends. I often go out with my friends, but sometimes I enjoy just reading in my room.

**3**

**A:** Do you plan to study abroad?

**B:** I haven't really decided yet. I guess I'd like to one day, maybe in Canada or Australia.

**4**

**A:** Do you have any brothers or sisters?

**B:** Well, I have one brother and one sister.

**5**

**A:** What's your job?

**B:** I have a part-time job in a local shop. In fact, I've worked there for more than three years.

**6**

**A:** Where do you live?

**B:** Actually, my parents moved around a lot and I've lived in many cities. Now I live in Osaka.

### 1.2

**1**

**A:** Yes, I have one sister. She's older than me. We have quite a good relationship now, but when I was younger it was different – not so good. We had to share a room and sometimes we argued about clothes and CDs – things like that. I guess that it's normal to fight a little with your sister.

**2**

**B:** Now I'm living in London, but before that I was studying in Ireland – for 2 years. Actually, it was great. I was living in the countryside and it was very peaceful. Not like London – it's so busy and noisy! I guess I'll get used to London eventually – it just takes time to adjust, doesn't it?

**3**

**C:** I enjoy playing most sports – especially team sports. Actually, I'm interested in learning the rules of cricket. It seems difficult to understand but I'd like to try it. I played baseball in Japan and I think it's similar. Also, I like playing soccer too, errr, you say football, don't you? But in fact ...

**4**

**D:** It depends. I enjoy speaking with my friends, but reading and writing I find difficult. Also, I have problems with vocabulary – I don't have enough! I've only been learning for one year, so I think I will continue to improve – I hope so.

**5**

**E:** Actually, I quit it last month. I was working as a nurse for a very long time, but now I want to study further because in the future I'd like to become a dentist. I'm not sure why I want to do this. Most people think I'm crazy, but teeth have always been very interesting to me.

**6**

**F:** Yeah, I want to go to Sydney in Australia. I want to study business there so I can run my father's business. But, actually, I'm more interested in Australia because the sun and the surfing is good and it's one of my hobbies. I will study hard too. I must work hard to get a degree in business – and then go to the beach.

# 2 Shopping and the Internet

### 2.1

(C = Customer; SA = Shop assistant)

**C:** Excuse me?

**SA:** Yes. Can I help you?

**C:** I want to buy a new camera.

**SA:** Certainly. Digital or film?

**C:** Digital.

**SA:** Any particular make or model?

**C:** No ... I've just started looking, actually.

**SA:** Well, this is the EazeeShot ZX. As you can see, it has a zoom lens ...

**C:** Mm. Looks good!

**SA:** Hmm. Takes good pictures too. In fact, you can store up to 5,000 photos in its memory.

**C:** Really ...?

### 2.2

**1** You will hear a man enquiring about buying a computer.

**2** You will hear a shop assistant talking to a customer about mobile phones.

**3** You will hear a woman complaining about a faulty radio.

### 2.3

**1**

(C = Customer; SA = Shop assistant)

**SA:** Good morning, sir. Can I help you?

**C:** Yes, I'm looking for a computer.

**SA:** Desktop, laptop or palmtop?

**C:** I'm not sure. A desktop, I think.

**SA:** All our desktops are over here. Now what kind of thing do you want to use it for?

**C:** Writing documents, mainly. My old one has just died!

**SA:** Well, I'm sure we can find you a replacement. And do you need a monitor as well?

**2**

(C = Customer; SA = Shop assistant)

**SA:** Good afternoon.

**C:** Hello. I was looking at your mobile phones ...

**SA:** Did you see anything you like? This one here is very popular. It has a full colour screen, a built-in camera and polyphonic ringtones.

**C:** Does it have video messaging?

**SA:** No. I'm sorry. Text and picture messaging only.

**C:** And which networks can I use it on?

**3**

(C = Customer; SA = Shop assistant)

**SA:** Yes, Madam? Can I help you?

**C:** I hope so. It's this radio. I bought it here a few weeks ago and it's stopped working.

**SA:** Oh dear! So what is the problem exactly?

**C:** Well, it's the volume control. It just doesn't work. No matter how much you turn it, it just doesn't get any louder.

**SA:** Hmm ... Could be the batteries.

**C:** No. I tried that. Still no good.

**SA:** OK. We'll let our workshops take a look at it. Now can I take down some details? Er, your name, please?

### 2.4

(C = Customer; SA = Shop assistant)

**SA:** Good afternoon.

**C:** Hello. I'm looking for a mobile phone.

**SA:** OK. Well, you've come to the right place. Did you want any particular model?

**C:** Well, it's a birthday present for <u>my son, George</u>.

**SA:** OK. And how old is he?

**C:** George? He's 13 next week.

**SA:** Ah! A teenager! Is this his first phone?

**C:** Yes. We want to be able to contact him when he's out and he wants to chat with his friends.

**SA:** Well, this phone is very good for texting, you know, sending SMS messages. It's got predictive text and all that. That's what all the teenagers want. They're text mad!

**C:** Really?! Is it expensive to send a text?

**SA:** Not as much as making calls. On this particular network, it only <u>costs 10 cents</u>.

**C:** 10 cents! That's pretty cheap.

**SA:** Yeah. Some networks are even cheaper.

**C:** Such as?

**SA:** Let me see ... At the moment <u>the cheapest network is ABC</u>.

**C:** ABC.

**SA:** Yeah. But, as with all networks, it depends what time you use it.

**C:** Oh really?

**SA:** On this network, the most expensive time is morning. But if you call <u>in the evenings, you can save the most</u>.

**C:** OK. I'll tell him that. By the way, how does he pay for the calls?

**SA:** Two ways. Contract, but he'd need a bank account for that. For teenagers it's best to have 'Pay As You Go'. This way you pay in advance for all your calls and you never get any nasty bills. You just have to buy a top-up card now and again.

**C:** Where can you buy those?

**SA:** Top-up cards? Most <u>newsagents and supermarkets sell them</u> these days.

**C:** Good. What about abroad?

**SA:** Sorry?

**C:** My son is going abroad on a school trip. They are going on a Mediterranean cruise. And they'll be stopping at lots of different countries. Can he use it in Europe?

**SA:** Sure. He can use it and buy top-up cards <u>in 120 countries worldwide</u>.

**C:** Fantastic! One last thing. We often go cycling in the mountains. What's the coverage like?

**SA:** It depends. This network is quite good. They say it <u>covers 87% of the country</u>, which isn't bad.

**C:** OK. I'll take it.

**SA:** Fine. Now, will you be needing a hands-free kit?

**C:** A what?

**SA:** A hands-free kit. It allows you to use the phone without using your hands. Basically, if he does a lot of cycling, it's much safer to be in control of your bicycle. This way he can make calls and still be in control. <u>It's much safer</u>.

**C:** OK. I'll have that too. Now how much is it?

### 2.5

(C = Customer; SA = Shop assistant)

**SA:** Now, sir. Have you thought about caring for your new computer?

**C:** Sorry?

**SA:** By taking out an extended warranty on your new computer, you don't have to worry about it breaking down.

**C:** That sounds good. Is it expensive?

**SA:** If you take it out at the same time as you buy your computer, we'll give you a 25% discount, which works out at £15 a month.

**C:** Sounds good. I'll take it.

**SA:** OK, let me just get the form. Now, sir. I need to get a few personal details. Could I have your name, please?

**C:** It's Banks. Jonathan Banks.

**SA:** Could you spell that for me, please?

**C:** Yes. It's Jonathan, J-O-N-A-T-H-A-N, Banks, <u>B-A-N-K-S</u>.

**SA:** Thank you. And that's Mr.

**C:** Doctor, actually.

**SA:** Really? Do you know, I've been having terrible pains in my lower back, I ...

**C:** I'm sorry. I'm not that sort of doctor ...

**SA:** Oh!

**C:** I'm a doctor of Philosophy.

**SA:** Oh, right, philosophy ... Address?

**C:** <u>17A, Leigham Street</u>, Newtown.

**SA:** 70 or 17?

**C:** 17. 17A, Leigham Street.

**SA:** Can you spell that for me, please?

**C:** Yes. It's L-E-I-G-H-A-M.

**SA:** OK. And do you know your postcode?

**C:** It's <u>NT3 5OP</u>.

**SA:** N-T-3, 5-O-P. And do you have a telephone number? Preferably a daytime number.

**C:** It's <u>01382 25669</u>.

**SA:** Erhuh ... And what about an email address? I presume you'll be keeping the same one.

**C:** Yes, It's <u>banks123@fastnet.com</u>.

**SA:** OK ... fine. One last thing. Do you want us to put your name on our mailing list to keep you informed of any new products or special offers?

**C:** I don't think so. <u>No. No, thank you</u>.

**SA:** OK ... How would you like to pay – cash, cheque, credit card or hire purchase?

**C:** Here's my card ...

### 2.6

(C = Customer; SA = Shop assistant)

**SA:** Yes, madam. How can I help you?

**C:** I want to buy a radio. It's a present for my daughter.

**SA:** One moment, madam. I'll show you what models we have in stock.

**C:** Thank you.

**SA:** This one's very popular, 'The Club Tropicana'.

**C:** 'The Club Tropicana'! It's certainly very colourful, isn't it?

**SA:** The colours are very popular with children. It comes in <u>pink, orange and green</u>.

**C:** Oh, yes. I think she'd like that.

**SA:** And it's got a CD player and <u>a clock</u>.

**C:** Does the clock have an alarm? My daughter is terrible at getting up in the mornings.

**SA:** Yes, it does.

**C:** It's a bit big.

**SA:** That's because <u>it has four built-in speakers</u>, madam.

**C:** How much is it?

**SA:** Well, it usually retails at $59.99, but it's on special offer this week, so I could let you have it <u>for 39.99</u>.

**C:** 39.99. Uhm. Not bad. Anything else?

**SA:** There certainly is. Introducing our top of the range model: 'The Night Owl'. Available only in black. But packed with extra features.

**C:** Such as?

**SA:** A clock. And it has <u>a television</u> complete with 10 cm screen. And, and this makes it perfect for the bedside table, a built-in reading light.

**C:** Very clever!

**SA:** Yes. It's ideal for use both indoors and out. <u>The batteries last for 100 hours</u>.

**C:** Sounds good. Who's it made by?

**SA:** <u>Parker</u>, madam. They're a British company. Very good quality.

**C:** Parker ... How much is this one?

**SA:** $79.99, plus tax.

**C:** That's a bit expensive. Do you have anything cheaper?

**SA:** Here. This is the cheapest, smallest and lightest one we do.

**C:** It's tiny! And it's round! That's really unusual.

**SA:** Yep. It's called '<u>The Olympic</u>'. You wear it round your neck with this special strap. See?

**C:** Oh! It's like a medal! An Olympic medal!

**SA:** That's why it's gold. And you get a free pair of headphones so you can listen to it wherever you are! And you never have to replace the batteries!

**C:** Really? Why not?

**SA:** There aren't any!

**C:** Oh?

**SA:** <u>It runs on solar power</u>.

**C:** Does it really? And I suppose it's expensive?

**SA:** <u>$18</u>, madam.

**C:** I'll take it.

**SA:** Certainly, madam. Now, cash, cheque or credit card?

## 3 Jobs and Job-hunting

### 3.1

**1**

**Student 1:** OK, let's see. The job I have at the moment is my first job. I am a waitress in a coffee bar. When I started, I only cleaned the tables. It was a little boring because I did the same thing all the time, but after a short time, I got a promotion – you know, a higher position. Now I make coffee and serve the customers at the cash register – it's more interesting. Would I do it in the future? I think, yes, why not? If I am a student, it is a good job to earn some money. The hours are very flexible – it is convenient in that way. What do I like? Hmmm ... Well, my colleagues are very nice, and so is my boss – they are very friendly. But what I really don't like is the uniform – it is a little stupid with this hat.

**2**

**Student 2:** Before I came back to my studies, I was a teacher in a primary school. My students were young – perhaps 5 or 6 years old. I taught students many many different subjects, for example, we studied reading and writing, and mathematics – errr, art and music, and others – but music was my favourite. I was a little like a mother in some ways – I listened to their problems sometimes. I enjoyed my job very much but now I want to change, I want to do something completely different in the future – but I'm not sure what exactly. I liked teaching very much – especially because I love children. But I did not like the administration. There were a lot of papers to write out everyday, and I'm not very good at office work.

**3**

**Student 3:** I used to be a chef in a kitchen in a busy restaurant. The restaurant was in a hotel and sometimes I cooked for 40 people, errr, guests in the hotel. I liked my job and would like to do it in the future, but especially if I could have my own restaurant. I liked it because it was creative and you could use your imagination, but the thing that I didn't like was it was very hard work. When I finished my work, I was usually exhausted. I was only able to go home and sleep ...

# 4 Crime and Punishment

### 4.1

(PO = Police officer; BW = Businesswoman)

**PO:** Yes, madam?

**BW:** Hello. Good morning, officer. I'd like to report a crime. A theft. My briefcase has been stolen. It's a black one. It's really important I get it back.

### 4.2

**BW:** It's really important I get it back. It had all sorts of things in it ... my mobile phone, some pens, a calculator. But the most important thing was some documents, a report for a client, the one I was going to meet. I must get that report back. It's extremely important.

### 4.3

**PO:** Now where was this bag stolen from?

**BW:** Well ... I had lunch at a French restaurant with a friend ... but I still had it with me when I left. I was on the way to an important meeting with a client. But on the way, I had to drop off a dress at the dry cleaner's ... And that's when it happened, when I took the dress into the dry cleaner's. I left my briefcase on the back seat of the car. And when I came out, it was gone.

### 4.4

**BW:** What time was the theft? Now, let me see, what time was this? We met for lunch at one o'clock. And left the restaurant at two. The dry cleaner's is quite close to the restaurant, so it must have been sometime around ten past two.

### 4.5

**BW:** I really don't understand how it could have happened. Honestly, I only left the car for about five minutes ...

### 4.6

**BW:** I don't know who could have taken it. The street was almost empty apart from one or two pedestrians. I did see a woman on a bicycle, but that was after I discovered the bag had gone. I do remember seeing a man sitting in a car parked opposite. He was just staring at me. And when I came out of the shop, he had gone. It must have been him. Really! These things wouldn't happen if we had more police officers on our streets.

**PO:** OK, madam. If I can just take down your name and address ...

### 4.7

(RA = Radio announcer; PO = Police officer)

**RA:** Coming up to 6.30 pm here on County FM. Time for our weekly 'County Crime Report'. Joining us now, our old friend Inspector Holland. Good evening to you, Inspector.

**PO:** Evening, Sue. Evening all. This week we'd like to ask listeners to help us with a particularly important crime – a burglary at the County Museum here in the centre of town. It involves the theft of several items of both local and national importance and despite having three of our most experienced officers on the case, we've very few leads so far.

What we do know is this. Sometime on Saturday night or Sunday morning, a gang of thieves broke in and stole several valuable objects. Firstly, an antique wall clock from the main gallery. Now, this clock is not only beautiful, it is also unique. In fact, it's the only surviving piece by the master clockmaker, George Mendelssohn. Consequently, it is worth a small fortune. In fact, it was last valued at £250,000.

The second item on the thieves' shopping list was a painting. A life-size portrait of local parliamentarian and anti-slave trade campaigner, Sir John Foxton. Now, those listeners who have visited the museum will almost certainly remember this painting. It's the very large painting of the man on the white horse.

And for those of you who don't know it, this is a particularly fine painting by the renowned 19th century artist Henry Radley and is valued at around half a million pounds.

Now, how the burglars managed to get into the building is <u>a mystery</u>. No windows were broken. Nor was there any sign of any doors or windows being forced open. The burglar alarm failed to go off. Now, it's not impossible that they had a key – several people have keys to the side entrance.

### 4.8

**PO:** As I say, unfortunately, we have had few leads on this case. However, a witness who lives <u>opposite the museum</u> has been able to give us some information about who may have been involved. Now, this lady was woken up at around 3 am on the night in question by <u>loud music</u> directly outside her window. On looking out of her window, she saw a man sitting in the front of a van, shouting, singing. Now, this man is described as having a big <u>white beard</u>. The witness said he looked 'a bit like Father Christmas'. As for the van, no positive ID on the make, as yet. But the witness described it as <u>blue or green</u>. So, were you in the area of the museum late on Saturday night? Did you see *anything* suspicious? If so, please help us put these precious items back where they belong and these criminals in prison. If you have *any* information, please call the police now on the free hotline. That's <u>0800 666 000</u>. 0800 666 000. That's it from me. Till the same time next week. Evening all.

**RA:** Our thanks to Inspector Holland there. You're listening to County FM. We'll be right back after this.

### 4.9

(D = Dave; A = Al)

**D:** Hi, Al!

**A:** Hi, Dave. Just working on our presentation for tomorrow. How's your bit coming along?

**D:** That's tomorrow? I thought it was next week.

**A:** You mean you've done nothing?

**D:** Look, Al, I've had a lot of things to do ...

**A:** OK. Don't worry. Sit down. This is what I think we should do. Firstly, let's give a few facts and figures about the crime rates here in London.

**D:** Like what?

**A:** Like in the last financial year, there were over

one million crimes reported in the Greater London area.

**D:** You're joking! Must have just been a bad year, right?

**A:** Well, it's <u>an increase of almost 23,000 on the previous year, so I'm afraid it's a rising trend</u>.

**D:** What sort of crimes? Murder?

**A:** Luckily, murder only accounted for a small percentage – under two hundred in total.

**D:** What about robberies?

**A:** Robberies totalled about 43,000.

**D:** 43,000! That an increase too?

**A:** <u>No, the previous year was almost 9,000 more</u>.

**D:** At least something's moving in the right direction. What about burglaries?

**A:** From homes or business premises?

**D:** Both.

**A:** Er ... let me see. <u>About the same the year before – 113,000</u>. But that's not including shoplifting.

**D:** What about cars? There must be loads of car crime.

**A:** Yeah, half a million vehicles are stolen in the UK every year. In fact, vehicle crime accounts for about <u>25% of all reported crime</u>. That includes thieves stealing things from cars too.

**D:** So, what do you want me to do?

**A:** Perhaps you could give the audience some details and then maybe some advice about how to prevent car crime.

**D:** OK. Look, I'll do some research and meet you after lunch.

### 4.10

**A:** So, what did you find out, Dave?

**D:** Well, if your car gets stolen, you'd think the police would find it eventually, wouldn't you?

**A:** I suppose so ...

**D:** Well, according to my research, <u>only 60% of cars are returned to their owners</u>.

**A:** 60%? What happens to the rest?

**D:** Who knows? And, listen, I thought it was safer to buy a second-hand car rather than a new one, right?

**A:** Yeah ...

**D:** Well, listen to this: '<u>Older cars have a higher probability of being stolen than new ones.</u>' Can you believe it?

**A:** So, any advice on preventing car crime?

**D:** Well, don't think that by parking in a car park your car is safe. <u>30% of all car crime happens in car parks</u>.

**A:** Yeah, I've been in some pretty scary car parks in my time.

**D:** Best to park it somewhere busy, and at night <u>choose a well-lit area</u>.

**A:** Makes sense. Anything else?

**D:** Never leave <u>the keys</u> in the car, not even for a second. Don't leave any cash, credit cards, cheque books, mobile phones, vehicle documents or anything, really, <u>where it can be seen</u>.

**A:** My dad had a hat stolen from the back of his car.

**D:** A hat?

**A:** Yeah. Baseball cap.

## 5 Transport and Inventions

### 5.1

**1**

(E = Examiner; C = Carlos)

**E:** What do you think would happen if cities stopped investing in public transport?

**C:** It would be a big problem.

**E:** For example?

**C:** <u>I think</u> workers would spend a lot of time travelling to work.

**E:** Would there be any other problems?

**C:** Yes, it wouldn't be good for business – companies want to invest in cities with good public transport.

**E:** How do you think transport will change in the next 100 years?

**C:** <u>I think</u> it will change a lot.

**E:** How?

**C:** Well, it will depend on a lot of things.

**E:** What might it depend on?

**C:** <u>I think</u> it depends a lot on what kind of technological developments happen over the next 100 years.

**2**

(E = Examiner; R = Raj)

**E:** What do you think would happen if cities stopped investing in public transport?

**R:** Well ... <u>I'd imagine there would be</u> a lot of problems. People would waste a lot of time travelling to and from work, which means that the city would not be a very enjoyable place to live in – people's quality of life would certainly get worse.

**E:** How do you think transport will change in the next 100 years?

**R:** Well ... <u>It's difficult to say, but maybe</u> with new technology people will work more and more from home, so they won't need to travel so much. In this kind of situation, <u>perhaps</u> transport won't need to change very much at all.

**3**

(E = Examiner; LL = Li Lin)

**E:** What do you think would happen if cities stopped investing in public transport?

**LL:** Mmm ... Well, <u>I think</u> people wouldn't be very happy! There would be more people in cars, more traffic jams and more pollution. Also, cities with poor public transport aren't very good places to do business in, so <u>I think</u> companies wouldn't go there.

**E:** How do you think transport will change in the next 100 years?

**LL:** Well ... <u>I think</u> people won't travel very much in the future because they'll be able to experience everything in virtual reality through computers. <u>I think</u> it might be like this computer game I was playing last week ...

### 5.2

(E = Examiner; C = Candidate)

**1**

**E:** What would you think if the government decided to stop people driving in city centres?

**C:** Mmm, well ... <u>I think it'd be a good idea</u> because there is <u>too much pollution</u> produced by cars and also there is too much traffic on the roads. In my home city there is a very good public transport system, for example, so people can always take the bus or subway.

**2**

**E:** Do you think the government should spend more money on building roads or railways?

**C:** Well ... people prefer taking their cars than taking the train, <u>so, for me, building roads is more important</u>. In my country, for example, <u>the trains are often so crowded that nobody really wants to go by train</u>.

**3**

**E:** Do you think we should increase the maximum speed limit for cars?

**C:** <u>Yes! I completely agree</u> – the speed limit is too low in towns and cities – especially at night when there is so little traffic and no children on the streets. Also, the motorway speed limit in Japan is crazy – I really think <u>we should do the same as Germany</u> and have no speed limits on motorways. It works fine there.

**4**

**E:** Some people say that car drivers should pay higher taxes if they have bigger cars. What would you say?

**C:** Yeah ... <u>I tend to disagree</u>. In my view, people should pay more tax because they earn more money, not because they have a bigger car. <u>Somebody could have a big *old* car which is very *cheap* – why should they pay more than someone with a small *new* car which is very *expensive*?</u>

## 6 The Natural World

### 6.1

**A:** I don't think it's right that animals are kept in captivity.

**B:** Doing tests on animals is morally wrong, I feel.

**C:** We are so wasteful! We ought to only eat produce from our own region at the time of year it is naturally available.

**D:** It's not my job to look after the environment. What do I pay my taxes for?

### 6.2

**1**

**A:** I don't think it's right that animals are kept in captivity.

**B:** Absolutely. I couldn't agree with you more.

**2**

**A:** Doing tests on animals is morally wrong, I feel.

**B:** Yeah, but a lot of important discoveries have come out of that research, you know ...

**3**

**A:** We are so wasteful! We ought to only eat produce from our own region at the time of year it is naturally available.

**B:** 'Naturally available'? I'm not sure I follow you ...

**4**

**A:** It's not my job to look after the environment. What do I pay my taxes for?

**B:** What!? You can't be serious! Don't you know every little bit helps?

### 6.3

(DB = Dr Bannister; C = Cedric; A = Amina;)

**DB:** Hello. For those who don't know me, my name is Ray Bannister. Anyway, welcome to today's Life Sciences seminar. Now, this term we'll be looking at the relationship between man and animals. Let's start by looking at zoos. Have you ever been to a zoo, Cedric?

**C:** Yes, lots of times. They used to take us on day trips when we were at school.

**DB:** And what do you think of zoos? Are they a good thing, do you think?

**C:** Oh, yes. All the lions and tigers and snakes. <u>It's great fun</u>.

**DB:** But many people are critical of zoos. Why is that – Amina?

**A:** Well, I don't like zoos. Zoos turn animals into a sideshow. Animals should be free to live their lives. If you put an animal in a cage, you take away its dignity.

**C:** Yes, but, Amina, zoos allow people to see and learn about animals.

**A:** That's true. But we can see animals and learn about them from the television.

**C:** But that's no substitute for seeing the real thing.

**DB:** OK. Let's look at other aspects of zoos' work. Is it not true that many zoos actually help to preserve some endangered species?

**C:** That's right. At my local zoo, you can help animals by adopting an animal. You get news on how it's doing and pictures and everything. <u>We sponsored an orangutan at my school</u>.

**A:** But some zoos actually make the situation worse by taking an animal out of the wild. Surely it would be better to leave it where it is?

**DB:** Well, Amina, that's not necessarily the case. <u>Many animals are hunted and many natural habitats are being destroyed</u> and if the animals were left there, they would die.

**C:** Yeah, and zoos run breeding programmes to increase the numbers of particular species.

**A:** OK. I agree. Zoos do some useful work. But <u>what upsets me is seeing those poor animals in those tiny cages</u>. They have no space to run around and they get stressed being kept in a cage all day.

**DB:** But in recent years many zoos have got rid of the cages and given the animals more space to move around. And then, of course, there are safari parks. Has anyone ever been to a safari park?

### 6.4

(E = Eddie; D = Dawn; F = Fran;)

**E:** Hi, Dawn.

**D:** Oh, hi, Eddie. How are you?

**E:** OK now. <u>Last month I was ill for several days</u> but I'm much better now.

**D:** What was the matter?

**E:** Well, the doctors weren't sure. They did several tests but couldn't find anything wrong with me. But I'm fine now. Look, can you spare a few minutes? <u>I'm doing a survey on people's attitudes towards vivisection</u>. It's for my assignment.

**D:** Yeah. OK. Oh ... this is Fran. She's in my study group.

**E:** Hi, Fran. I'm Eddie. Pleased to meet you.

**F:** Hello, Eddie.

**D:** What's it about again?

**E:** Vivisection. You know, doing experiments on live animals. Are you for or against vivisection?

**D:** <u>Well, for, I suppose</u>.

**E:** OK. That's one for ...

**F:** You don't mean you support vivisection, Dawn? It's horrible what they do to those poor animals.

**D:** But new drugs and treatments have to be tested, Fran. I mean, you couldn't ask a person to take a lot of untested drugs. They might die.

**F:** But that's just it. A person could refuse. People have the right to choose what they want to do, and so should animals.

**E:** So, you think animals should have rights?

**F:** Yes. <u>Animals have just as much right to life as we have</u>, and they have the right to be treated well, you know, and not abused in this way.

**E:** You obviously feel quite strongly on this. What about you, Dawn?

**D:** In a perfect world, I'd agree with you, Fran. But it's not a perfect world. For example, take your mystery illness, Eddie. Perhaps animal research could help with that.

**F:** Yeah, but he's better now.

**D:** That's not the point. What if he was an old man or a small child? Some people might not get better as easily as he did.

**F:** What's that got to do with keeping animals in tiny cages in a lab and performing lots of horrible experiments on them? Do you know they force dogs to smoke? It's horrible.

**D:** It may be horrible, Fran, but the fact is that the research could save lives. You know, <u>great advances in Alzheimer's disease have been made through animal research</u>.

**E:** OK, but do you think all animal research is valid, Dawn?

**D:** What do you mean?

**E:** Well, just because something works with a rat or a monkey doesn't necessarily mean it works on humans. We're different physically. So, do you support all animal experiments?

**D:** Well, I ...

**F:** <u>And as for testing cosmetics on animals</u>! Do you know they deliberately put shampoo into rabbits' eyes just to see what happens? I mean,

**who** needs a new shampoo? The ones in the shops work just fine.

**D:** Um, yeah, I take your point ...

**F:** What's more, we don't need to use animals these days. Medical technology is so advanced, they can use computer simulated models or cell research. They don't need a whole animal.

**D:** Well ... That's true ...

**E:** OK. Thank you both very much. You've given me some really interesting ideas. Bye now!

**D:** Any time.

**F:** Bye.

### 6.5

(T = Teacher; D = Donna; K = Kyle)

**T:** Good afternoon, everyone. This week's presentation is from Donna and Kyle. Ready?

**D,K:** Yes. Just about ...

**T:** OK. Away you go. And we'll do a q and a when you finish.

**D:** Good afternoon. Even as children, most of us can recognise some of the cat family: the tiger with his stripes; the leopard with his spots; the lion with his mane. But how much do we really know about them and their behaviour? Let's look at three quite distinct members of the cat family. First, the only one of our three cats not endangered – the lion, the king of the jungle. Why is he the king? First, his sheer physical presence. An adult male can weigh anything between 160 and 250 kilograms. No wonder they're called big cats! Secondly, there may be heavier or even bigger animals on the plains of Africa, the elephant, for example, but when it comes to hunting and killing, few can match the lion.

**K:** Actually, the male is not the biggest predator. It's the female, the lioness.

**D:** That's right. Lionesses often work in small groups, usually two or more, to corner and kill their prey – gazelle, zebra, wildebeest or buffalo.

**K:** But when the lionesses are off hunting, who looks after the cubs?

**D:** Ah hah, it's the females again! Rearing the cubs is a shared responsibility for the females of the pride.

**K:** So, if the lionesses kill most of the food and look after all the cubs, why is the male king of the animals?

**D:** Good question, Kyle.

**K:** Yes ... well, moving on from the king of the animals to the fastest – certainly on dry land.

**D:** The cheetah. A truly beautiful creature. Unfortunately, endangered and nearly extinct.

**K:** Built for speed, its greyhound-like body is very light for its size, weighing merely 30 to 50 kilograms. Its long tail gives it its distinctive shape and helps it balance better when it's on the move.

**D:** Cheetahs are found in Africa, the Middle East and South Central Asia. Unlike the lion, cheetahs are usually solitary hunters, though they will occasionally work in groups in order to bring down larger prey such as buffalo. Other prey include springbok, warthog and gazelle.

**K:** What's most impressive about the cheetah is its speed. It can reach a speed of a hundred and ten kilometres per hour in only a matter of seconds.

**D:** Finally, the ocelot, one of the smallest of the 'Big Cats'. There, isn't he cute? They weigh as little as 6 kilograms – that's only as much as some domestic cats. Sadly, the ocelot too, is threatened with extinction through habitat loss and being hunted for its beautiful fur. It is found in most South American countries with the exception of Chile, and also in Central America and some southern US states.

**K:** The lion and the cheetah both live and hunt in open plains. The solitary ocelot prefers to live and hunt in forests. Here they catch rodents, reptiles and even fish.

**D:** Uhm ... They have an interesting technique for fishing, too, using their paws to flip fish out of the water and then pounce on them.

**K:** So, there you are, three quite distinct but all equally amazing members of the cat family.

**T:** Fascinating! Any questions?

## 6.6

(W = Wayne; B = Becky)

**W:** Hi, Becky.

**B:** Oh! Hi, Wayne. You weren't at the Environmental Studies lecture this morning ...

**W:** No, I er ... Did I miss anything?

**B:** 'Factors influencing river life' and Doctor Bellamy set us an essay.

**W:** Oh no!

**B:** Don't worry. I took some notes. Now, listen carefully. A river's speed will dictate which animals and plants can survive in it. Got that? Usually, the faster the water, the more oxygen it contains. That's good for life. But fast-flowing rivers are more difficult to swim in, so some animals prefer more mature, slower rivers.

**W:** Slower rivers ...

**B:** Now, on its journey from its source to the sea, a river may pass over several different types of substrate: clay, sandst ...

**W:** Substrate?

**B:** The layers of rock beneath it. Clay, sandstone, chalk, soft or hard limestone, etc. Anyway, each kind of rock has an influence on the mineral content of the water and the species of animals and plants that are able to survive there.

**W:** Er, mineral content?

**B:** For instance, the freshwater crayfish requires water with plenty of oxygen and a good supply of lime to help create and maintain its thick, outer skeleton. So, a fast-flowing river running over chalk is perfect.

**W:** Chalk, right ...

**B:** Another factor is man. In the past, some rivers have been used as transportation channels by large industrial boats. In fact, some still are. So, many stretches of river have had to be deeply dredged – dug out – to maintain a deep channel. This prevents the bottom of the river developing naturally.

**W:** Right ...

**B:** What's more, smaller craft need water plants such as lilies, reeds and rushes to be removed ...

**W:** Otherwise they get all caught up in the propellers!

**B:** That's right! But their removal means that there is less habitat for wildlife. What's more, fast motor boats create wash that causes the erosion of the river banks, floods the nests of animals and washes away wildlife.

**W:** That's terrible! All those little water rats and birds!

**B:** The last main factor, Wayne, is pollution.

**W:** I never drop any litter; I ...

**B:** Unfortunately, it's not people like you or me that are mainly responsible for river pollution.

**W:** No?

**B:** The commonest kinds of pollution are industrial and include sewage; chemicals and other waste created by industry; fertilisers and pesticides; litter; large amounts of hot water; dense or decaying plant growth and, finally, slurry – that's animal waste.

**W:** Animal waste. Right. Thanks, Becky. When's this essay got to be in?

**B:** Friday.

**W:** Friday! Guess I'd better get to the library.

## 7 Food and Diet

### 7.1

**Candidate:** Well, the last time I ate at a restaurant was about two weeks ago, when I went to a fast food place in Oxford Street with my girlfriend. It was early in the evening, about six o'clock, and Oxford Street was very busy. It was also very wet because it was raining heavily ... and we didn't have an umbrella!

Anyway, I'm a vegetarian, so I had a veggie burger with French fries and a large chocolate milkshake which was SO good ... and only cost about £4. My girlfriend, Tomoko, had a salad and a bottle of mineral water because she doesn't like the type of food they have there. She didn't say anything but I don't think she liked the salad very much because it was covered in a very oily dressing. She was pretty angry by the end of the meal.

### 7.2

**Student A**

1 How would you define a healthy diet?

2 What do you think are the reasons why many people do not eat healthy food?

**3** How can governments encourage people to eat more healthily?

### 7.3

**Student B**

**4** Are fast food companies responsible for making people fat?

**5** Why do you think fast food is so popular?

**6** What would happen if restaurants had to label all their meals to clearly show ingredients, calories, fat content, etc.?

## 8 Sickness and Health

### 8.1

In today's Architecture & Society lecture, we look at hospital design. Now, one of the first modern hospitals was the Hospital de Sant Pau in Barcelona, Spain, which was designed by the Catalan architect Domenech I Montaner and completed in 1930. As you can see, the hospital is built on a large, square site, surrounded by a wall. The buildings are laid out on the diagonal. The main entrance is in one corner, at the bottom of the plan here. You enter through this large building, which is also the main Administration Block. Behind this are two parallel rows of smaller buildings, or pavilions, each dedicated to a separate function. For example, the first on the right is the Intensive Care Unit. Opposite that is the building for Digestive Disorders. The third building on the left is the Obstetrics and Gynaecology Unit, for women's health care. After that, also on the left, are the laboratories. At the end of this avenue of pavilions is a large building with two wings. This is the Faculty of Medicine and incorporates the Blood Bank and Radiography Unit.

### 8.2

Around this central avenue are other buildings. On the left, in the middle, we find the Psychiatric Block, where patients with mental problems are treated. Now, Domenech had great attention to detail, he even created a house specifically for storing medical records. It's that small building there, near the centre of the wall on the left.

Moving round, we come to this long building, which dominates this part of the site. This is the Surgery Block, where most of the major operations take place. Moving round again, the building to the right of

the avenue is the Paediatrics Unit. This is where babies and children receive treatment. Finally, in this right hand corner, we have the 'Casa de Convalecencia' or House of Recovery. This was where you stayed if you were not confined to bed, but were still not quite well enough to go home. These days it is not part of the hospital, but is used by a university language department.

Domenech's radical approach to hospital design was a major step forward in health care, but what else have architects done to improve our health?

### 8.3

But I'm pleased to report that no fatalities occurred in the accident. The schoolchildren only suffered minor injuries – cuts and bruises – and the bus driver, who sustained a compound fracture of the patella of his right leg, is now up and about – though he still needs support to walk.

### 8.4

Good afternoon, ladies and gentlemen. Welcome to Medical School. First, let us remind ourselves of the reason we are all here – the human body.

The human body survives on air, food and water. These are processed by several organs, which are all located in the main, central part of the body, which is known as the torso. Today we've only got a plastic model of a human torso. You'll have to wait a while before we let you get your hands on the real thing!

OK, let's look how this thing works. Air enters the body through the mouth and nose and is carried to the lungs through the trachea, commonly known as the windpipe. The lungs – and there are two of them, one on the left, one on the right – take oxygen from the air and put it into the blood. This oxygen-carrying blood is then pumped around the body by the heart, via a series of tubes known as arteries and veins. Please note the location of the heart. It is in the centre of the chest, not on the left as we often imagine!

Now, in the lower part of the torso, the abdomen, we find a series of long tubes. These are your intestines, and again you have two of them: a small intestine and a large intestine. The job of the intestine is to absorb nutrients from food you have eaten earlier and collect waste material before it is excreted. It usually takes food about 24 hours to pass through the intestine.

Above the intestine is the liver. The liver is a large organ and has the important job of separating toxic from useful substances. <u>The kidneys remove waste and pass it into the urine</u>. The kidneys are located behind the intestine – and I think you can just see them at the back at either side there. Down at the bottom here, we have <u>the bladder, a kind of bag where urine is collected</u>. The bladder is emptied of urine when we urinate.

OK. Any questions so far?

### 8.5

Now, let's look at some basic emergency procedures. First, fainting. Someone has fainted and they are lying flat out on the floor. What's the first thing to do? Answer: If necessary, roll them over so they are <u>lying on their back. Raise both their feet above the level of the head</u>. Why? To increase the blood circulation to the brain. Secondly, make sure their breathing passage is clear. Do this by <u>turning the head to one side and tilting it back</u>. If the fainting attack lasts for more than a few seconds, place the person in the recovery position, which is done like this ...

### 8.6

While I remember ... As medical students, you'll be regularly visiting – and working in – hospital wards. Now, you will be expected to wear a white coat. If you don't have one, you'd better get one.

I also strongly suggest you buy yourself the following items: A notebook. You are going to be getting an awful lot of information thrown at you over the next few years. Make sure you keep good notes. Obviously, you'll be needing a pen. A thermometer is always useful for taking a patient's temperature, as is a watch for checking their pulse. <u>Please don't bring your mobile phone with you</u>, as they can interfere with some of the equipment. Finally, if you haven't bought your own stethoscope just yet, don't worry – the department will supply you with these. One last thing. Please don't drive to the hospital, you will certainly find it impossible to park anywhere nearby. One or two students have tried to park in the ambulance bays and have got into all sorts of trouble. <u>Please use public transport</u>.

# S A M P L E

## BRITISH COUNCIL

**IELTS** idp AUSTRALIA

**UNIVERSITY of CAMBRIDGE** ESOL Examinations

PENCIL must be used to complete this sheet

Centre number:

Please write your name below.

then write your six digit Candidate number in the boxes
and shade the number in the grid on the right in PENCIL.

Test date (shade ONE box for the day, ONE box for the month and ONE box for the year):

Day: 01 02 03 04 05 06 07 08 09 10 11 12 13 14 15 16 17 18 19 20 21 22 23 24 25 26 27 28 29 30 31

Month: 01 02 03 04 05 06 07 08 09 10 11 12    Year: 00 01 02 03 04 05 06 07 08 09
Last 2 digits of the

## IELTS Listening Answer Sheet

| | ✓ 1 ✗ | | 21 | ✓ 21 ✗ | |
|---|---|---|---|---|---|
| 1 | | | 21 | | |
| 2 | 2 | | 22 | 22 | |
| 3 | 3 | | 23 | 23 | |
| 4 | 4 | | 24 | 24 | |
| 5 | 5 | | 25 | 25 | |
| 6 | 6 | | 26 | 26 | |
| 7 | 7 | | 27 | 27 | |
| 8 | 8 | | 28 | 28 | |
| 9 | 9 | | 29 | 29 | |
| 10 | 10 | | 30 | 30 | |
| 11 | 11 | | 31 | 31 | |
| 12 | 12 | | 32 | 32 | |
| 13 | 13 | | 33 | 33 | |
| 14 | 14 | | 34 | 34 | |
| 15 | 15 | | 35 | 35 | |
| 16 | 16 | | 36 | 36 | |
| 17 | 17 | | 37 | 37 | |
| 18 | 18 | | 38 | 38 | |
| 19 | 19 | | 39 | 39 | |
| 20 | 20 | | 40 | 40 | |

Checker's Initials    Marker's Initials    Band Score    Listening Total

IELTS L-R v4.0    DP500/392

---

# S A M P L E

Are you:   Female?    Male?

Your first language code:

## IELTS Reading Answer Sheet

Module taken (shade one box):    Academic    General Training

| | ✓ 1 ✗ | | 21 | ✓ 21 ✗ | |
|---|---|---|---|---|---|
| 1 | | | 21 | | |
| 2 | 2 | | 22 | 22 | |
| 3 | 3 | | 23 | 23 | |
| 4 | 4 | | 24 | 24 | |
| 5 | 5 | | 25 | 25 | |
| 6 | 6 | | 26 | 26 | |
| 7 | 7 | | 27 | 27 | |
| 8 | 8 | | 28 | 28 | |
| 9 | 9 | | 29 | 29 | |
| 10 | 10 | | 30 | 30 | |
| 11 | 11 | | 31 | 31 | |
| 12 | 12 | | 32 | 32 | |
| 13 | 13 | | 33 | 33 | |
| 14 | 14 | | 34 | 34 | |
| 15 | 15 | | 35 | 35 | |
| 16 | 16 | | 36 | 36 | |
| 17 | 17 | | 37 | 37 | |
| 18 | 18 | | 38 | 38 | |
| 19 | 19 | | 39 | 39 | |
| 20 | 20 | | 40 | 40 | |

Checker's Initials    Marker's Initials    Band Score    Reading Total